Excel Macros

Comprehensive Beginners Guide to Get Started and Learn Excel Macros from A-Z

TABLE OF CONTENTS

Introduction

If you have multiple tasks in Microsoft Excel which are to be performed repeatedly, then you may record a macro for automating the tasks. The macro is an action or a bunch of actions which you will be able to run as many times as you wish. While you are creating a macro, you are recording the mouse clicks and keystrokes. It is an automated sequence used as an input which imitates mouse actions or keystrokes. The macros are typically used as replacements for the repetitive series of mouse and keyboard actions. They are used commonly in word processing and spreadsheet applications such as MS Word and MS Excel. The file extension used for the macro is .MAC.

Macro is a code which automates work in programs as they allow you to add your own little features and improvements to aid you in accomplishing what is needed fast and with the click of a single button. For the spreadsheet applications such as Excel, a macro is typically very powerful. The word macro has meanings in other fields. To macro means keeping track of the number of carbohydrates, proteins, and fats consumed on a specific day. Physique competitors such as bodybuilders master this art and have no qualms about whipping the food scale at any given instant.

The general-purpose macro processor or a universal purpose preprocessor is called a macro processor which is not connected to or integrated with any specific language or piece of software. The macro processors are programs which copy a piece of text from one place to another thereby making a systematic set of replacements in the process.

There are many ways in which the macro is run in MS Excel. It is an action or a set of actions which can be used to automate some tasks. The macros are recorded in VB (Visual Basic) for an application programming language. You may always run macros by clicking the macro command on the Developer tab on the ribbon.

1

Macro is a tool which permits you to add functionality to the forms, controls, and reports in addition to automating the tasks. For instance, if you add one command button to your form, you are associating that button's OnClick event to the macro and the macro has the necessary commands for performing every time the button is clicked.

When you consider Access, think of the macros as a basic programming language which you write by developing a list of actions to perform. Once you have developed a macro, you can choose the action from a dropdown list which appears and fill out the required info for every action.

The macros empower you to add functionality to the reports, forms, and controls without having to write codes in Visual Basic for VBA Applications module. They provide a subset of commands which are available in VBA. This simplifies the job for most people who find it easier to build macros instead of writing VBA codes.

For instance, let's say that you wish to begin a report directly from one of the data entry forms. You may add one button to your form and then develop a macro which starts the report. Macro may either be a standalone entity (an object in the database) that is tied to the OnClick incident on the button, or macros may be embedded directly on the OnClick event of the button which was a new feature of Access 2007. In any event on the click of the button, the macros run and start the report.

Chapter 1

Macro Names

Understanding macro names

This term macro is commonly used for referring to specific macro objects viz; the objects you can observe under the Macro heading of the navigation pane. However, in reality, one macro object consists of several macros. In which case it is referred to as a macro group. This macro group gets displayed on the navigation pane as a standalone macro object however, the macro group really consists of more than a single macro. Of course, you can create every macro as a separate object but more often than not it is required that you group many related macros into single macro objects. The names in the Macro Name column identify every macro.

The macros contain independent macro actions. Most actions need more than a single argument. Additionally, you may assign names for every macro in the macro groups and you may add certain conditions to control how every action is performed. We will see these features in greater detail later.

If your macro objects contain just a single macro, there is no need for macro names. You may refer to the macro by the names of the macro objects. But when a macro group is involved, you need to assign a specific name to every macro. If the Macro Name column is invisible to the Macro Builder, click on Macro Names in Show/Hide group of the Design tab. For more info about running macros of the macro group, read on.

The macro names are a shortened method of referring to the macro expansions. This macro name is one unique string which begins with a letter or a special symbol such as @, #, or $. The macro name can have alphanumeric characters or the earlier mentioned symbols. It is recommended that you begin a macro name with @ while using Oracle. Although it is significant that macros should have unique names inside a specific application, the local and global macros can have the same name. In this case, the local macro will take precedence. For creating or referring to an application level local macro, use a double name such as Sample.'@JSUM'. Any portion of the macro name that has special characters needs to be enclosed in quotation marks (They could be single or double.).

Syntax:

- Syntax for application level local macro: name1.name2

- Syntax for a global macro: name2.

Here name1 is the name of the application and name2 is the name of the macro.

Arguments

The arguments provide a value to the action like what string is to be displayed in a message box, what control is to be operated on and so on. Some of these arguments are necessary while others are optional. Arguments can be seen in the Action Arguments pane which is below the Macro Builder. Arguments column was a new feature to Office Access 2007. It allows you to view and not edit the action arguments on the same line as that of the action. It makes things easier to read as far as macro is concerned as there is no need to choose every action to display the arguments. In order to display the arguments column, you must click the Arguments from the Show/Hide group which is on the Design tab.

Chapter 2

Macros and VBA

Difference between Macros and VBA

VBA (Visual Basic Applications) and macros are not exactly one and the same thing even though they are closely related, and many times they are used interchangeably. As we know, VBA is a programming language that may be used in many programs that are part of MS Office such as PowerPoint, Word, Excel, and Access. Macro on the other hand is not a programming language as explained by John Walkenbach in his book "*Excel 2013 Bible*". He is one of the best authors in the world of Excel and he explains that, macros are a sequence of instructions which automate certain aspects of Excel. In other words, the macro is a set of instructions which you wish Excel to follow to achieve some specific goal. VBA is a programming language which can be used to create the macros. For instance take the example of the following set of instructions:

The complete set of instructions is similar to that of an Excel macro. It is a set of instructions which should be followed in order to achieve a specific goal, that in this case is having a tsukemen meal. The language used for writing these instructions is English and is equivalent to VBA in the case of macros. Therefore, as you can see VBA and macros have a close relationship but technically speaking, they are not the same. But there are many terms which can be used interchangeably with the macros.

Macros vs. VBA - Why Macros?

Macros have been in use as a development tool for a long time since the MS Office product line was introduced. The macros incorporate generalized DB functions by using existing MS Access capabilities. The errors presented in the macros can easily be resolved by using the Help function provided by Microsoft. The Erase function which enables you to generate macros makes the development of macros appear simple and easy to accomplish.

The database operations and commands can be used to generate macros in the Macros window. These macros may be converted into MS Access VBA. Only some minor edits are required in most cases to the saved code to create a functional program. All the syntax, functionality and spacing is included in the saved file that contains VBA code particular to the specific application being recorded. Even the unskilled programmers can interpret the code and learn to generate the code and accomplish specific tasks. In this process, the new programmers can gain a useful introduction to VBA code. Building macros will always be simpler and quicker than writing VBA code especially for simple applications and for making global key assignments. However, it is not so easy for the complex and more advanced applications.

Most people consider macros because VBA code is considered to be more program oriented and it offers a range of options which appear confusing at times and difficult to understand. However, these options also provide the developer the opportunity to use the tools to extend the Access capabilities beyond what is packed officially with the MS Access software. Although building macros or generating them is easy and does not use up a great deal of time, you might want to consider their applications specifically if you wish to perform some simple tasks. If if you find macros time consuming and tedious as many have confessed, you should try and develop VBA code. By learning and building upon VBA skills, you develop programming skills so useful you can use them in several other applications. Macros, on the other hand, are useful in many applications but are specific to those applications. Macros are not portable to other applications that do not support them.

VBA is one of the easiest programming languages to learn. It does not need the knowledge of complex programming techniques used to program C++ or other higher level languages. VBA gives a user-friendly and form-based interface for assigning variables and make code development easy. VBA is the more widely used application which is available on a range of resources. The second party would have to know and understand the specific application in order to assist you in building a macro. VBA can perform all the operations that macros can perform and some more such as,

- Integrating Excel and Word features in the database.

- Incorporating the error handling modules to assist in running the applications.

- Process the data in the background.

- Provide the users with form-based professional layouts to interface with the DB.

- Perform conditional looping.

- Create multi-purpose forms.

Chapter 3

Why you should learn writing VBA macros in Excel

Excel macros save you a huge amount of time with automation of Excel processes which are used often. But in reality, the macros are pretty limited. And it is easy to make mistakes while using the recording tool as the recording process is a little awkward. If you use VBA for creating macros, it provides you with a great deal of additional power. You can instruct Excel exactly what to do and how to go about doing it. This way, you have access to more capabilities and functions. If you are required to use Excel regularly, it is worth learning about creating VBA macros.

As we have learned, VBA is a programming language that can be used in several Microsoft applications. Visual Basic or VB is the programming language and VBA is an application specific version of the language. Although MS discontinued VB back in 2008, VBA is going strong yet. Luckily for the non-programmers and beginners, VBA is pretty simple and the interface that is used to edit it provides a lot of assistance. Some of the commands you will use come with pop-up suggestions and automatic completions and this is extremely useful in getting your script working quickly.

However, VBA takes a little bit of time getting used to. If VBA is tougher than just recording a macro, why should you use it? The answer is that you get much more power out of using VBA macros. Rather than clicking around the spreadsheet and recording all the clicks, you are able to access Excel full range of functions and other capabilities. However, you must know how to use them. But once you are comfortable with the use of VBA, you can perform all the tasks you would in regular macros and that too in a lot lesser time.

The results will be a lot more predictable as you are telling Excel exactly what it should be doing and there is no question of any ambiguity at all. When you have created your VBA macro, it is simple to store it and share with someone who can take advantage of it. It is typically useful while you are working with many people who have to do the exact same thing in Excel.

VBA Macro in Excel! An example

Let's take a look at a straightforward macro. The spreadsheet contains some names of employees, store number where they work, and their quarterly sales figures.

	A	B	C	D	E
		Name			
1	Name	Store	Sales		
2	Renato Zold	4	$12,748.12		Store 1:
3	Kristi Mateo	4	$48,796.15		Store 2:
4	Filia Richfield	3	$24,855.21		Store 3:
5	Sigismondo Boadby	4	$21,688.44		Store 4:
6	Ivonne McTaggart	1	$41,197.66		
7	Luise Sannes	3	$34,319.93		
8	Georgi Denge	4	$19,168.85		
9	Pavia Tarburn	3	$34,126.50		
10	Joeann Antonetti	3	$31,270.43		
11	Jeannie Seviour	3	$32,145.24		
12	Livvyy California	4	$21,062.03		
13	Miles Ingry	3	$46,436.34		

The macro will add the quarterly sales of each store and assign the totals to corresponding cells in the spreadsheet. You can also find out about accessing VBA dialog online.

```
Sub StoreSales()


Dim Sum1 As Currency

Dim Sum2 As Currency

Dim Sum3 As Currency

Dim Sum4 As Currency


For Each Cell In Range("C2:C51")

        Cell.Activate

        If IsEmpty(Cell) Then Exit For

        If ActiveCell.Offset(0, -1) = 1 Then

          Sum1 = Sum1 + Cell.Value

        ElseIf ActiveCell.Offset(0, -1) = 2 Then

          Sum2 = Sum2 + Cell.Value

        ElseIf ActiveCell.Offset(0, -1) = 3 Then

          Sum3 = Sum3 + Cell.Value

        ElseIf ActiveCell.Offset(0, -1) = 4 Then

          Sum4 = Sum4 + Cell.Value

End If

Next Cell
```

Range("F2").Value = Sum1

Range("F3").Value = Sum2

Range("F4").Value = Sum3

Range("F5").Value = Sum4

End Sub

Although it may look long and complex, it can be broken into segments so that you can see the individual elements and learn about VBA basics.

Declare the Sub

At the start of this module, there is "Sub StoreSales()". It defines a new sub called StoreSales. You may also define various functions. The difference being, a function can return a value and sub cannot. If you are familiar with some programming languages, you will know that subs are the equivalent of methods. Anyway, in this case, we are not required to return a value so we are using a sub. At the end of the code, there is "End Sub" and it tells Excel that we are finished with VBA macro.

Declare variables

In the first line of the code in the script, there is "Dim". It is VBA's command for declaring variables. So "Dim Sum1" develops a new variable "Sum1". But we need to instruct Excel about the kind of variable it is. There is a need to select a data type. There are many kinds of data types in VBA. You can find a full list online. As this VBA macro will be dealing with currencies we will be using the Currency data type.

This statement "Dim Sum1 As Currency" instructs Excel to create a fresh currency variable "Sum1". Each variable you have declared needs to have one "As" statement so that Excel can identify the type.

Start a for loop

Loops are one of the most powerful entities you can create by using any of the programming languages. If you are not familiar with loops, you can find some online tutorials explaining the Do-While loops. Here we are using the "For" loop for our example. Here is an example of the "For" loop,

> For Each Cell in Range("C2:C51")
>
> [a bunch of stuff]
>
> Next Cell

The code orders Excel to iterate through the different cells in the scope we specify. Here we have used the Range object and it is a specific kind of object used in VBA. While we are using it like this - Range("C2: C51") - it tells Excel that we are interested in the 50 cells. The "For Each" tells Excel that we are going to do something with every cell in that range. The "Next Cell" comes after everything has been done and tells Excel to begin executing the loop from the start beginning with the next cell. There is also the statement: "If IsEmpty(Cell) Then Exit For.". It does exactly what it says. Conservatively speaking, in this case, using a While loop might have been a better choice but for the sake of teaching, let's settle for the "For" loop having an exit.

If-Then-Else statement

The base of this macro lies in the If-Then-Else statements. Here is the sequence of conditional statements,

```
If ActiveCell.Offset(0, -1) = 1 Then

    Sum1 = Sum1 + Cell.Value

    ElseIf ActiveCell.Offset(0, -1) = 2 Then

    Sum2 = Sum2 + Cell.Value

    ElseIf ActiveCell.Offset(0, -1) = 3 Then

    Sum3 = Sum3 + Cell.Value

    ElseIf ActiveCell.Offset(0, -1) = 4 Then

    Sum4 = Sum4 + Cell.Value

End If
```

You can mostly guess by reading the code what these statements do. However, it is possible that you are not conversant with ActiveCell.Offset. The "ActiveCell.Offset(0, -1)" tells that Excel to look for the cell that is one column to the left of the active cell, which is the reason for the minus sign. In this case, it is like telling Excel to consult the column called store number. If Excel finds a 1 in the column, then it will take the content of that active cell and add it to Sum1. If it finds a 2, it will add the content of the active cell to Sum2 and so on.

Excel will go through all the statements in a certain order. If the conditional statement is satisfied, only then will it complete the Then statement. If it is not satisfied, then it moves to the next ElseIf statement. If it goes all the way to the end of the code and not a single condition is satisfied, it will not commit to any action. A combination of conditional statements and the loops drive this macro. The given loop tells Excel to go through every cell that is selected and the conditionals tell it what to do with the cell.

Write Cell Values

In the end, we get to write the results of our efforts with the cells. Here is the code used to do that,

Range("F2").Value = Sum1

Range("F3").Value = Sum2

Range("F4").Value = Sum3

Range("F5").Value = Sum4

By using the .Value and the equal to sign, we are setting every cell to the value of the corresponding variable. And that is that. We inform Excel that we are done writing the Sub by using "EndSub" and this VBA macro is done. When we run this macro by using the Macros button in the Developer tab, we will get the desired sums.

	A	B	C	D	E	F	G
C51			f_x	35971.43			
1	Name	Store	Sales				
2	Renato Zold	4	$12,748.12		Store 1:	$452,782.74	
3	Kristi Mateo	4	$48,796.15		Store 2:	$208,489.37	
4	Filia Richfield	3	$24,855.21		Store 3:	$553,009.11	
5	Sigismondo Boadby	4	$21,688.44		Store 4:	$303,942.69	
6	Ivonne McTaggart	1	$41,197.66				
7	Luise Sannes	3	$34,319.93				
8	Georgi Denge	4	$19,168.85				
9	Pavia Tarburn	3	$34,126.50				
10	Joeann Antonetti	3	$31,270.43				
11	Jeannie Seviour	3	$32,145.24				
12	Livvyy California	4	$21,062.03				
13	Miles Ingry	3	$46,436.34				
14	Idaline Agates	1	$19,108.78				
15	Shirl Tarver	3	$23,445.03				
16	Jillene Krysztofowicz	3	$25,365.15				
17	Dickie Urwen	1	$40,528.21				

Building blocks of VBA in Excel

If you look at VBA macro above, it will appear a bit complex. However, after breaking it down into constituent parts, its logic becomes easy to understand. Similar to any scripting language, it will take some time to get used to VBA syntax. However, with practice, you can build up VBA vocabulary and you will also be able to write the macros faster and more precisely. You will also find more power than while using them with the recording method.

If you get stuck in any case, you can find all VBA answers on Google search as it is a simple and quick way of getting all the info. You can also find references online which are helpful if you are willing to dig through them for the right technical answer. When you are comfortable with the basics, you can begin to use VBA for things such as exporting Outlook tasks, sending emails via Excel, and displaying the PC information.

Chapter 4

Creating Macros
in 7 easy steps!

Do you keep track of the time you have to spend working on Excel on relatively unimportant, repetitive and small tasks? If you do and even if you haven't so far, you must have noticed that the routine stuff such as inserting standard text or formatting normally takes up a significant amount of time. Although you might have some practice of carrying out the activities and you are capable of completing them pretty fast, it is annoying to spend those five minutes each day inserting the company name and details in all the Excel worksheets you send to the counterparts or clients. It adds up over a period of time.

Although not in all cases, but in most, investing time on these common and repetitive operations does not yield proportional results. As a matter of fact, most of them are great examples of the 80/20 principle. They are a part of the majority effort which has little to no impact on the result. As you are a reading a book on Excel macros, you are probably aware of how the macros are one of the most powerful features of Excel. Also that they can aid you in automating the repetitive tasks.

So for this purpose, you are probably searching for a beginner's guide that explains the process in a simple way. Although it is easy to record the fundamental macros, it is an advanced subject and if you are looking to become an advanced programmer, you will come up with some complex material. So remember, some of the training resources in the tutorial are difficult to follow. However, it does not mean that the whole procedure to learn macros is impossible to actually learn. As a matter of fact, in this tutorial, we will see how to start to create macros in 7 easy-to-follow steps.

In addition to taking you through the procedure of setting up the macros step by step, the chapter will include a practical example. To be more precise, in the Excel tutorial we will see how to set up a macro which will perform the following duties,

- Type this in one of the active cell, "Here is the best Excel E-book." This is just an example and you can change it to the exact text you wish.

- Auto fit the width of the column of this active cell in a way that the typed text fits into a single column.

- Give the active cell red color.

- Change the active cell's font color to blue.

The Excel macros tutorial here is for beginners and it doesn't end here but is followed by additional information about Excel and macros. You can go through the e-book to find more. The 7 steps explained below are enough to set you up for developing fundamental Excel macros. But if you are looking to unleash the full power of MS Excel macros by using VBA, you will need to learn some advanced topics such as,

- Introduction to Visual Basic Applications (VBA) and the VB Editor (VBE).

- Explanation of how you can see the real programming instructions of the macro and how to use them to start learning about writing Excel macro codes.

- Learn about some tips which you can start using now in order to improve and accelerate the learning process of VBA programming and macros.

Make the Developer tab visible before starting to create macros

When you are ready to create the first macros, you will have to begin with some preparations. Before creating the actual macro, ensure that you have the necessary tools. In MS Excel, the most useful commands while working with the macros and VBA are on the Developer tab. By default, the Developer tab is hidden in Excel. So unless you or someone else adds the Developer tab to the Ribbon, you need to make Excel show it in order that you have access to the required tools while setting up the macros.

In this section, we will see how to add the Developer tab to the Ribbon. At the end of the explanation, you will find an image displaying the complete process. Make a note that there is only the need to display the Developer tab once for Excel. This is of course assuming that the setup is not changed or reversed later. Excel in such case will continue to display the tab for future opportunities.

1. Step 1: Open the Excel options dialog by using one of the following ways,

Method 1:

- Step 1: Right click on the Ribbon by using the mouse.

- Step 2: Excel will display a context menu.

- Step 3: Mouse click on "Customize the Ribbon".

Here is the image illustrating the 3 steps above,

Method 2:

- Step 1: Click on the tab called File Ribbon.

- Step 2: On the left side of the screen there is a navigation bar. Click on "Options" in it.

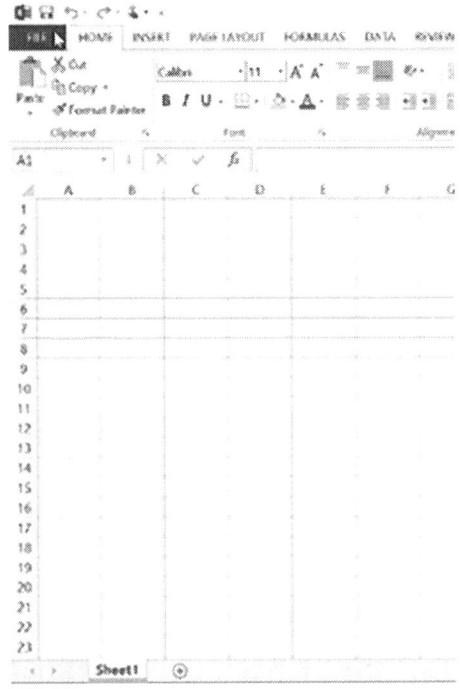

Method 3: You can use keyboard shortcuts for this like, "Alt+T+O" or "Alt+F+T".

2. Step 2:

When you have reached the Excel Options dialog, make sure that you are on to the Customize Ribbon tab by clicking the tab on the navigation bar situated on its left side.

3. Step 3:

Have a look at list box Customize the Ribbon. This list box is situated on the right side of the Excel Options dialog and find the "Developer". The "Developer" tab by default is the 3rd tab from the bottom of the list and it is just above the "Add-Ins" and the "Background Removal". The box on the left of the "Developer" is empty by default. So in this case, this "Developer" tab does not appear in the Ribbon. If the box has a check mark, the "Developer" tab will appear in the Ribbon.

4. Step 4:

If the box on the left of "Developer" is empty, click on it for adding a checkmark. If the box is already checked, there is no need to do anything. You must already have Developer tab present in the Ribbon.

5. Step 5:

Click on the OK button which is provided in the lower right corner of your Excel Options dialog. It will take you back to the worksheet and you will see the Developer tab appearing in the Ribbon.

Tools for creation of Excel Macros

Excel permits you to create the macros with the use of either of these following tools.

- First is the macro recorder that allows you to record the actions to be carried out in the Excel workbook.

- Second is the VBE (Visual Basic Editor) that requires you to write instructions that you wish Excel to follow in the programming language VBA.

This second option is far more complex than the first as it requires programming especially if you are a newcomer to this world of macros and do not have previous programming experience. As this book is aimed at beginners, we will see how to record macros using recorders. If the objective is only to record and later play the macros, this chapter will cover all the essentials required to support you to achieve this goal.

Walkenbach explained in his book *Excel 2013 Bible* that if your objective is only to record and playback the macros then there is no need to be concerned with the language; although a basic understanding of how things are done will be helpful. But if you are looking to really benefit from the macros and use its full power, you must learn VBA eventually.

It is observed by Bill Jelen and Tracy Syrstad who are both known Excel experts that, recording a macro is helpful for the beginners who have no experience in macro programming however, as you acquire more knowledge and experience you will start to record lines of code less often. Therefore the topics related to VBA programming are deeply covered in another chapter. Let's see how to record Excel macros using the recorder.

On the lower right corner of the Excel Options dialog, there is an OK button. This will take you back to the worksheet where you were working earlier and the Developer was appearing in the Ribbon.

The seven easy steps to create your first macro

Okay. Here you are. By now you must have added the Developer tab to your Excel Ribbon and must be aware that there are two different kinds of tools you may use for producing macros including using the recorder.

When you are ready to create the first macro, do it by simply using the seven steps explained below.

Step 1: Click on your Developer tab.

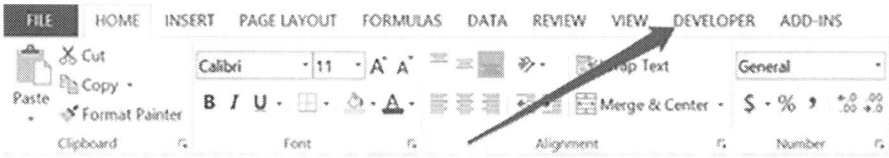

Step 2:

Make sure that the relative references recording is on by checking the "Use Relative References". If it is not, click it on.

If the relative references is turned on, there is no need to click anything as can be seen in the screenshot below.

The use of relative and absolute references can be explained later. For the moment, make sure that the relative references recording is turned on. If this is turned off (it is off by default) the exact cell locations are recorded in the macro. On the other hand, when the relative references is turned on, the actions recorded by Excel are relative to the active cells. In other words, as explained by Bill Jelen in Excel 2013 in Depth, the actual recording is extremely literal.

For instance, let's assume that you are creating a macro that types "A great book on Excel" in the Excel active cell. Then it copies the text which you have typed and paste it in the cell which is immediately below. If at any time during the recording the active cell happens to be A3 and you have failed to turn on the relative recording, the macro will record that it needs to type "A great book on Excel" in the active cell. Copy this text and paste it in the cell A4 which happens to be right below the active cell at the instant when the macro recording began.

As you might well imagine, the macro does not work well when the text is in any other cell than A3. Following images show what this looks like if you are working in cell H1 and activate the macro recording along with absolute references as explained above.

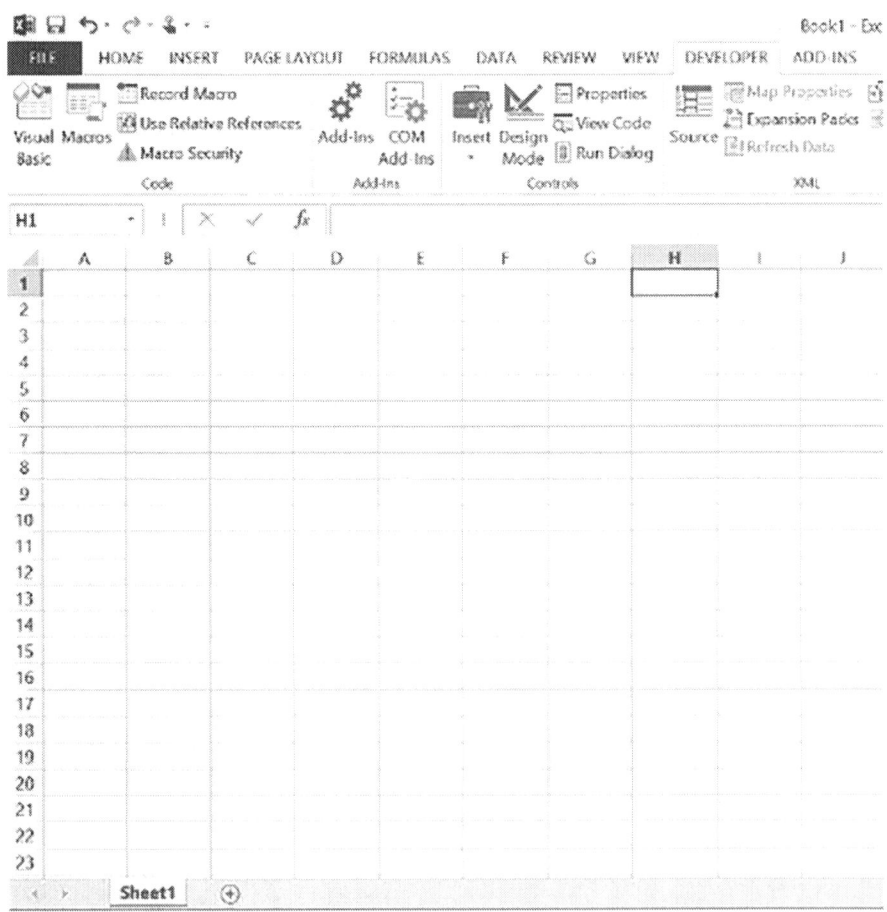

Step 3:

Click on the "Record Macro" on Developer tab or you can use the Record Macro button which appears on the left side of your Status bar.

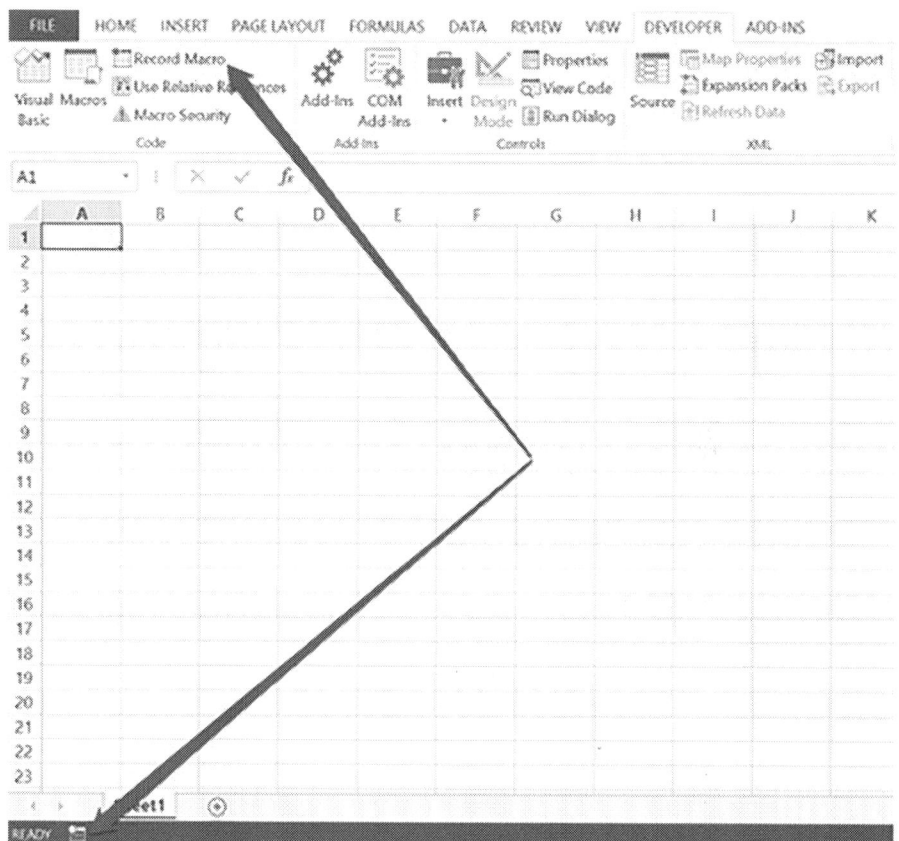

Step 4:

Now the Record Macro dialog will appear. It allows you to affix a name to the macro. Excel affixes a default name to the macro such as "Macro1", "Macro2", or "Macro3" etc. But as illustrated by Walkenbach in the book *Excel VBA Programming for Dummies*, it is wiser to use more descriptive names. The main rule for macro name is that it must begin with a letter of underscore (_) and not a number. You can't have special characters except the underscore or spaces and the names should not conflict with the existing names. For example, although "Best Excel Tutorial" will not be an acceptable name, "Best_Excel_Tutorial" will work.

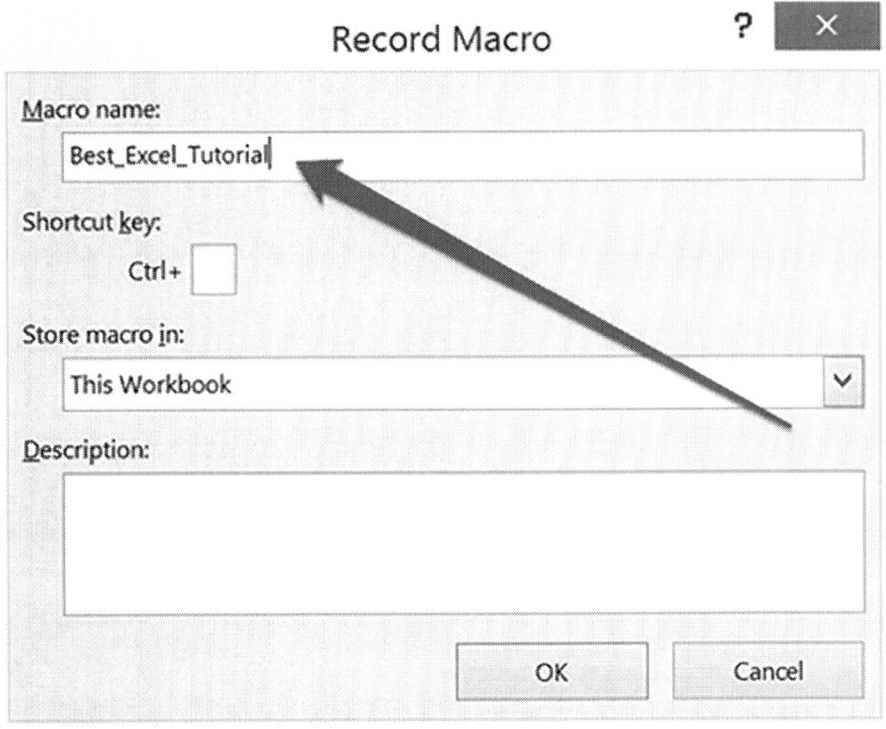

Assign the keyboard shortcut to macros

This is optional. You may set up a macro not having a keyboard shortcut. However, selecting the keyboard shortcut allows you to complete the macro execution by just clicking the selected key combination. The keyboard shortcuts to be assigned are in the form of "Ctrl+key" combination. This key combination could either be just a single letter (i) by itself or a combination of a letter and a Shift key. While creating keyboard shortcuts for the macros, you need to be careful about the exact key combinations you will select.

If you select a keyboard shortcut which has been assigned prior for instance to a built-in keyboard shortcut, your selection of keyboard shortcuts for the Excel macro disables and overwrites the prior existing shortcut. As Excel comes with several built-in shortcuts on the keyboard of the kind, "Ctrl+Letter", there is a risk involved in disabling the built-in shortcuts. For instance, take the example of the shortcut "Ctrl+B". Now it is a built-in keyboard shortcut for Bold command. Now if you affix the shortcut "Ctrl+B" to some specific macro, the built in keyboard shortcut used for the Bold command gets disabled. As a result, when you press "Ctrl+B" the macro will get executed but the selected text will have a bold font.

There is a way to address this issue and it normally works. This way is to assign shortcuts which are of the form "Ctrl+Shift+Letter". The risk involved in disabling and overwriting prior existing keyboard shortcuts is small but in any event, you need to continue being careful about the key combinations you select. For example, rather than choosing the "Ctrl+B" for the keyboard shortcut you could opt for something similar yet different in "Ctrl+Shift+B".

Record Macro	?	X

Macro name:

> Best_Excel_Tutorial

Shortcut key:

> Ctrl+Shift+ B

Store macro in:

> This Workbook ▼

Description:

>

OK	Cancel

Decide where you wish to store your macro. You may store the macro in your workbook which you are working with currently or on the new Excel file or in the personal macro workbook. The by default selection is to store these macros in a workbook that you are using. In such an event, you will be able to utilize the macro when the particular workbook is open.

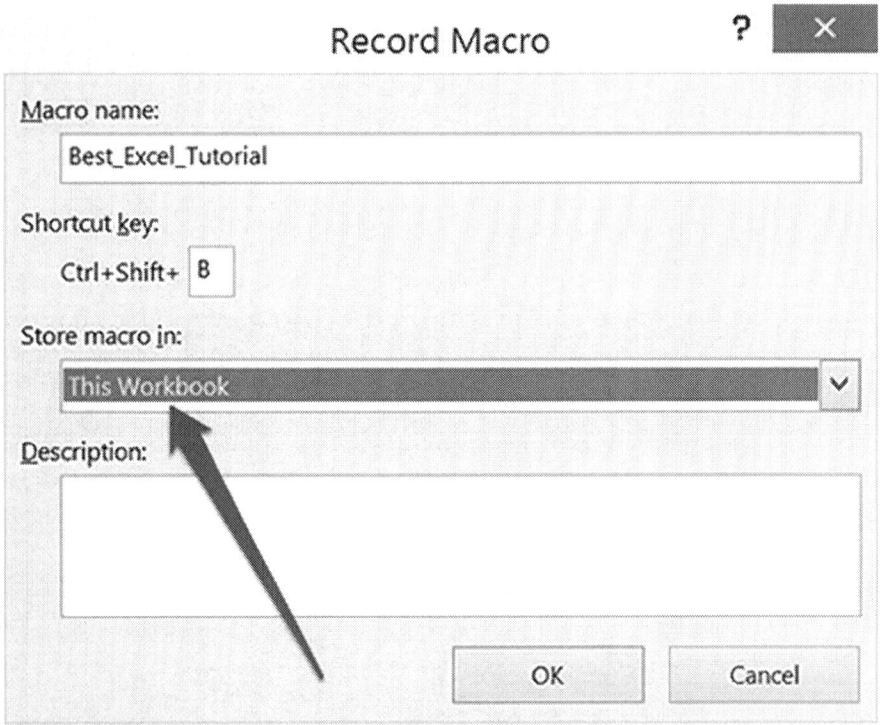

If you select "New Workbook" Excel will open a new file. You will be able to record and save a macro in the new workbook. However, similar to the case in which you select "This Workbook" the macros only work in the file where it was recorded. There are more advanced storing options available such as "Personal Macro Workbook". Bill Jelen defines the Personal Macro Workbook in his book Excel 2013 in Depth as a specific workbook designed to hold the general-purpose macros which might apply to any workbooks.

The main advantage to saving the macros in the PMW is that they can be used later in the future Excel files as the macros are available while

28

you are using Excel in the same machine where you recorded and saved them. It doesn't matter whether you are working on new or different files to the ones that you developed while creating the macros.

Create the Macro Description

Keeping macro description is optional but as described by Greg Harvey in his book on Excel, it is always a good idea to be in the habit of recording the info each time you build new macros so that you and the coworkers may know what to expect from the macros once you run them. He also suggested that you also include the date on which the macro was saved and also the name of the person who created the macro.

Step 5:

So now you have assigned a name, the location of the macros is set where you wish to store them and you have assigned a keyboard shortcut and finally created a macro description. Now click on the OK button for closing the Record Macro dialog.

Step 6:

Do the activities you wish the macro to record and save.

Step 7:

Click the "Stop Recording" on the tab Developer or you can also click the Stop Recording Macro button which appears on the status bar's left side.

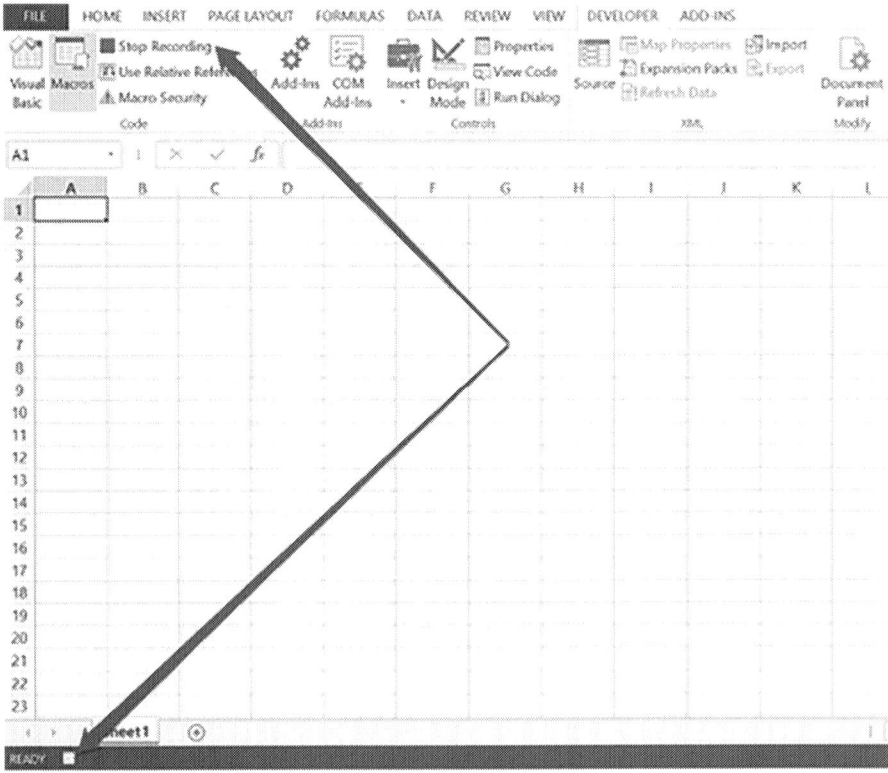

After completing the recording of your new macro, you can run it by using the keyboard shortcut which was assigned in the ctrl+shift+B. With your gradual experience increasing, you will find that there are many other ways of executing the macros like the macro above.

Hopefully, by reading this chapter you found it easy to develop and run your first macro. At least you must have realized by now that the basics of Excel macros are simple and not as difficult or complex as they might appear at first sight. The macro we have recorded by using the description above is a very basic example and other more deeper and complex topics involving VBA are dealt elsewhere in the book. They also allow you to set up and create more powerful and complicated macros.

But it is a fact that the information you have read and learned about is sufficient to set up a wide range of Excel macros. This is explained by John Walkenbach in his book *Excel 2013 Bible*. He said that in most cases, recording your actions as macros and then just replaying them doesn't warranty the knowledge of any code that gets generated. Therefore you have learned the first part totally.

Chapter 5

Beginning the writing of Excel macro code

We have seen how to set up the macros in Excel and as you must have observed in the recent sections, these macros are running. For starting to learn how to program macros, it is needed that you take a look at the actual code or instructions behind what you have recorded as the macro. For this, there is a need to activate the VBE (Visual Basic Editor). First, open the VBE by clicking on the "Visual Basic" on the Developer tab or by using the keyboard shortcut "Alt+F11".

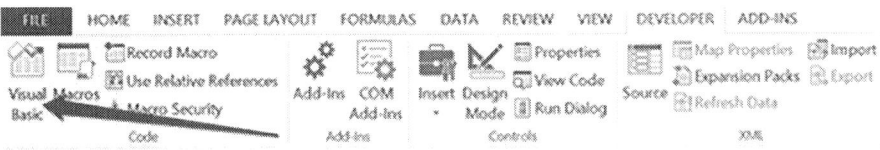

This way, Excel will open the VBE that looks like this,

Remember VBA window can be customized, therefore it is possible that this window that gets displayed in your computer is slightly different than the screenshot. The first time it was seen there were two questions in the writer's mind,

1. What am I looking at?

2. Where is the code for my macro? (This is a more pertinent question)

As you may have the exact same questions, we will answer them. What is it you need to look for in the VBE (Visual Basic Editor)? There are six main sections in which the VBE is divided.

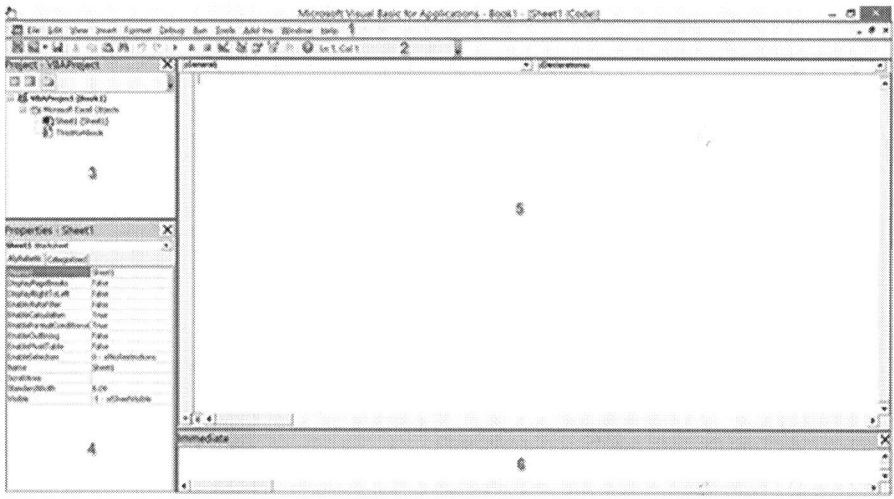

Section 1: Menu Bar

The VBE menu bar is like any other menu bar which you get in other programs. More precisely, this menu bar contains some drop-down menus in which you can find most commands you can use to provide instructions and interact with the VBE. When you are working with the more advanced versions of Excel such as those after Excel 2007 and later, you would have noticed that Excel itself does not come with a menu bar rather, it has a Ribbon. And the reason behind it is that from MS Office 2007 onwards, the company has decided to replace the menu and toolbars for some programs with Ribbons.

Section 2: Toolbar

This VBE toolbar, much similar to the VBE menu bar, is like any other toolbar you could encounter while using another type of software. To be more accurate, this toolbar contains items like on-screen buttons, menus, icons, and other similar elements. This toolbar shown in the screenshot above is standard and it is a default toolbar for the VBE. John Walkenbach explains in his book *Excel VBA Programming for Dummies*, that many people including the writer himself just leave the toolbars as they are.

As indicated above, if you have a later version of Office (later than 2007) you will not see either a toolbar or a menu bar in the Excel window as MS has replaced them both with Ribbons.

Section 3: Project Window or Project Explorer

Project window or the project explorer is a part of VBE where all the open Excel workbooks are displayed and the add-ins are loaded. The section is extremely useful for navigation. As you may observe in the screenshot below, the VBE permits you to either expand or collapse different sections of the list just by clicking on a + or - (depending on the case) which is displayed on the left-hand side of the appropriate branch.

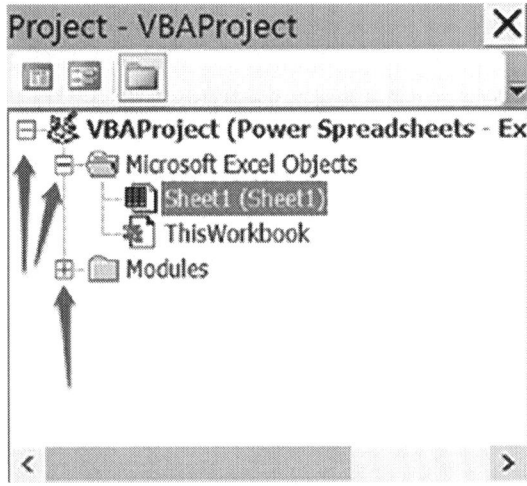

When VBA Project gets expanded, it shows different folders which are loaded at that moment. There could be many folders for different kinds of items like objects, sheets, modules, and forms. What these terms mean will be explained in other portions of the book. Once a folder gets expanded, you will be able to see the different individual components in the folder. For instance, in the screenshot above, there are two folders MS Excel Objects and Modules and MS Excel Objects folder that appear expanded and has 2 items Sheet1 and This Workbook. If you are unable to see the Project Explorer, it is probably hidden. In order that Excel shows the Project window, use "Ctrl+R" keyboard shortcut. Then click on Project Explorer icon within the toolbar or you can go to the View menu and click on "Project Explorer".

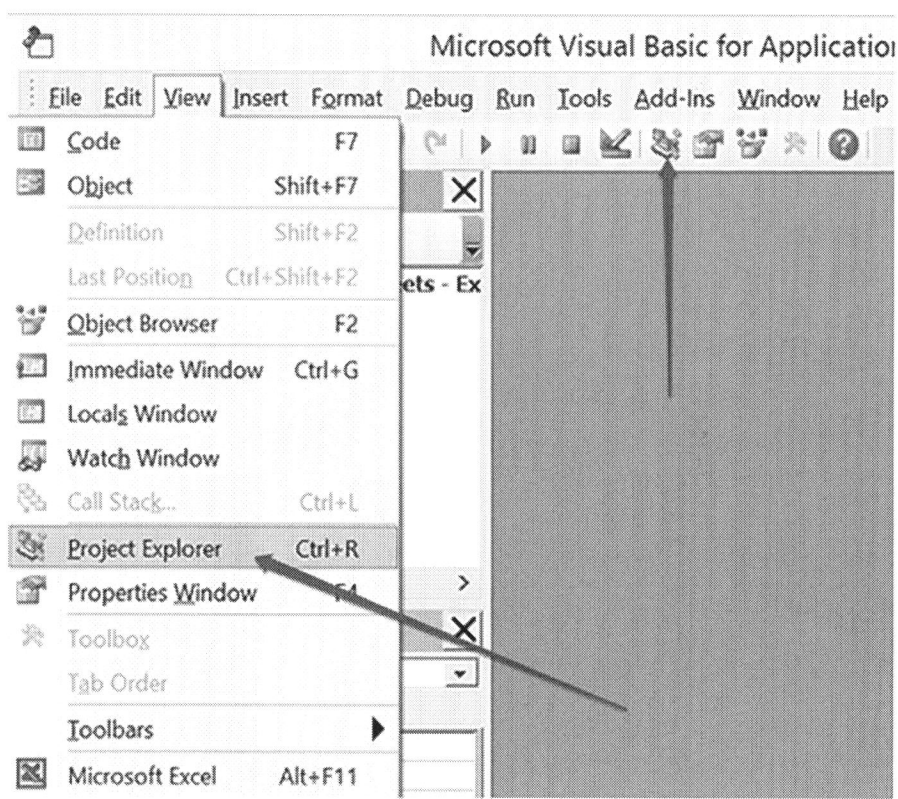

Section 4. Properties Window

In the Properties Window section of the Visual Basic Editor, you can edit the item properties or properties of anything you might have selected in the Project window. You can either hide or unhide this Properties window. If the VBE is not displaying the Properties window at a particular moment, you can use F4 which is a keyboard shortcut to click on the Properties window icon of the toolbar or expand the View menu to click on the Properties window.

Section 5: Programming window

When you have recorded a macro, it is in the Programming Window where the code will appear. We will see the explanation about how to get the VBE to display the macro's code in the next section. Apart from displaying the code, this Code Window is the place where you may actually write or edit VBA code.

Section 6: Immediate Window

The main use of the Immediate Window is for the purpose of noticing errors, debugging and checking. You might have noticed that in the very first screenshot of the Visual Basic Editor which has been included above, you cannot see the Immediate Window. There are two reasons for this. First is that this window is hidden by default. The second as explained by Walkenbach is that the window is not very useful for beginners and so it might be the reason behind keeping it hidden. In order to unhide the Immediate Window, you can use "Ctrl+G" keyboard shortcut or access View menu and click on the "Immediate Window".

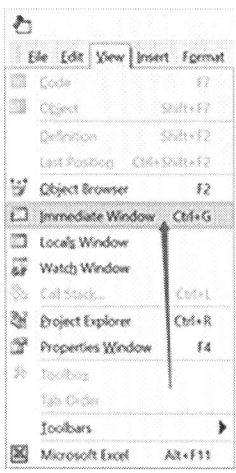

Now that you are aware of what to look at while working with the VBE, let's move ahead and learn about how you can actually see the code of the macros you have developed.

Where is VBA macro code located?

Project Window is the section of the VBE that is normally used for navigation purposes. Let us go back to it and take a closer look at the screenshots below.

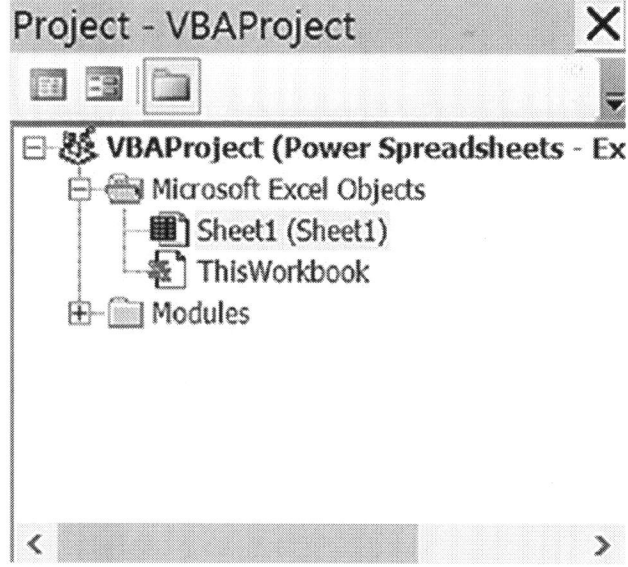

In this screenshot above, when you expand the "VBA Project" it will show two folders MS Excel Objects and Modules. You may look at the elements included in the first folder (MS Excel Objects) however not in the second which is Modules. For expanding the Modules folder and check its components, you have to click on "+".

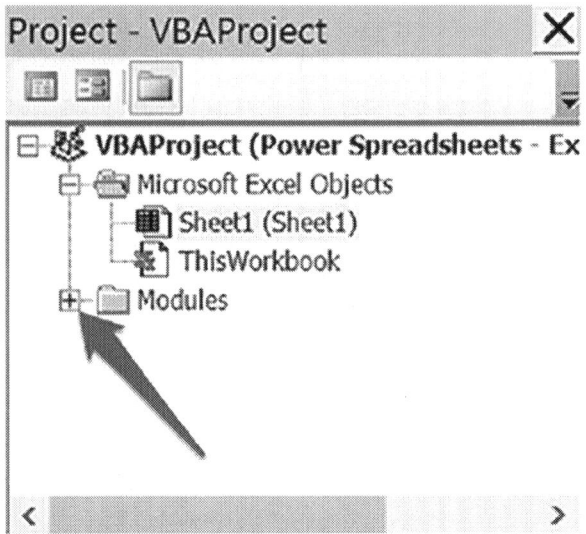

The Project Explorer looks like this,

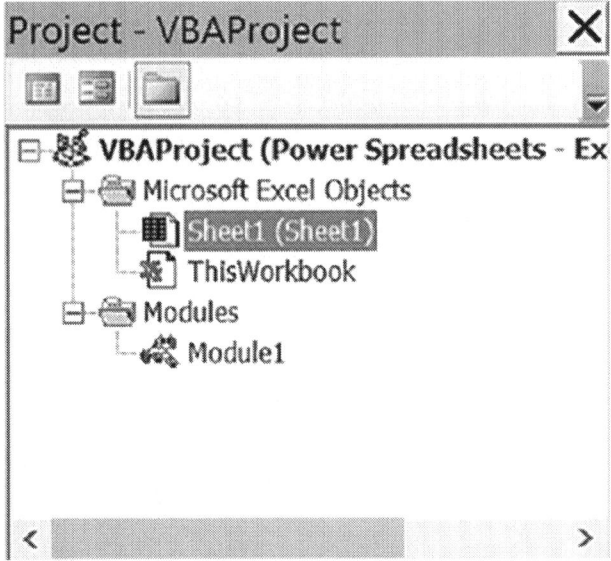

The items which appear in the MS Excel Objects folder might appear familiar but you may think, what is a module? The module in the words of Walkenbach is a container for VBA code. In other words, it is the place where VBA code actually gets stored. When you have recorded your first macro, you can observe that the macro code gets stored in a module which is Module1.

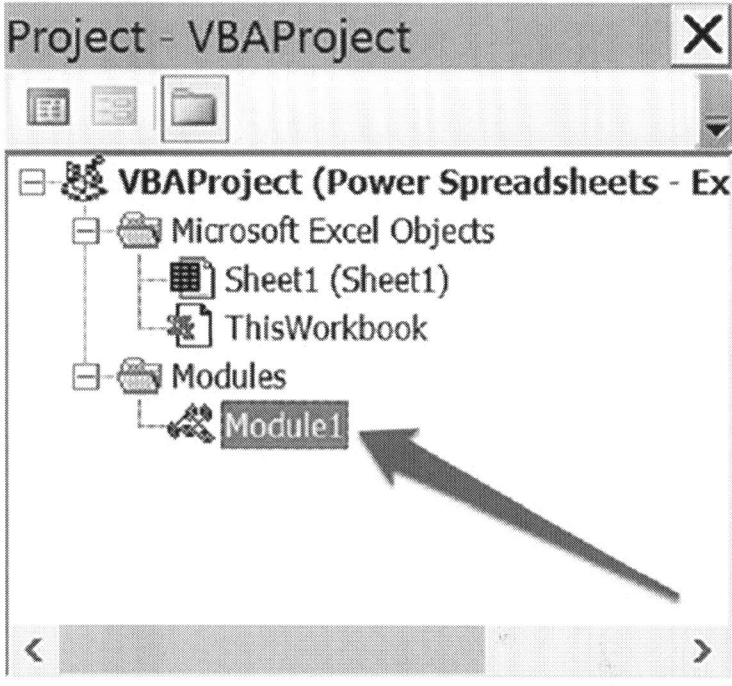

In order to have the VBE displaying VBA code you can double click on Module 1 or right click on Module1 and then select View Code.

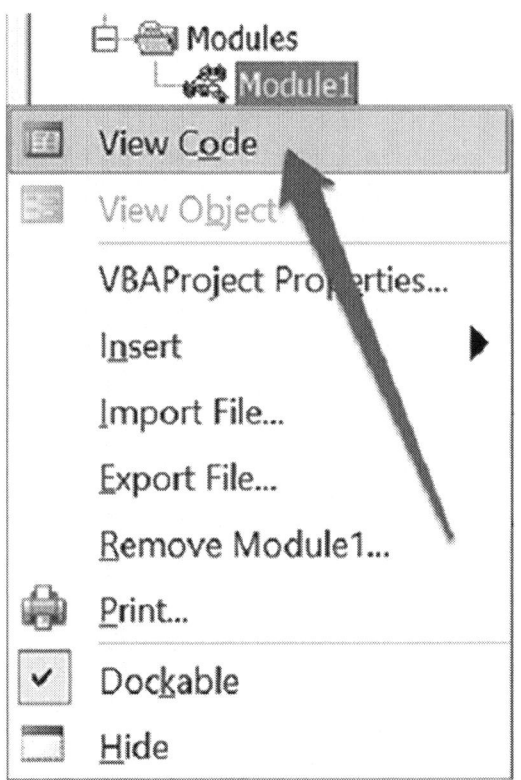

And now, the VBE will display the macro code in the programming window. If you have recorded a macro by using the example given in the earlier chapter, you would have created a macro, Best_Excel_Tutorial and your code will roughly look like this,

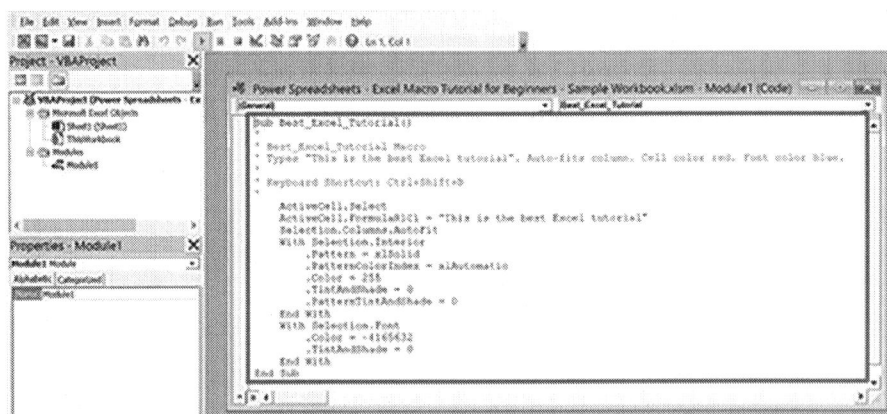

Now the next question is, does that code make any sense? The good part is that yes it does a bit at least. But you will probably feel that you are not completely understanding the instructions in the Excel macro you have created. The second thought which is natural to have come to your mind is that why such simple events like writing some text, coloring cells, auto-fitting columns and changing the font color require such elaborate coding? It is a natural query and we will take a closer look at the macro code to make sense of the whole thing.

Using the basic Excel macro code for learning VBA from scratch

The good thing to know as you may have noticed is that VBA code is kind of similar to English. In his book *VBA for Excel Made Simple*, Keith Darlington who is an experienced programming teacher has explained how the structured English that is similar to common English will be helpful in understanding the instructions. It will help while thinking about the instructions macros need to follow before actually writing them down for VBA.

So, you can understand some of the words and also some instructions along with them. For instance, you will probably identify or even partially understand some of the following lines from the macro recorded earlier for the beginners,

What is ActiveCell.Select?

The active cells are the cells that are currently selected in the worksheets. It is assumed here that even if you are not an expert on VBA or Excel, you will know the term "select". As you can imagine, the piece of code chooses the currently active cell.

What is Selection.Columns.Autofit?

The line of code again begins with a selection. But it is referring to the columns and auto-fitting. If you can recall from the previous chapter, the 2nd thing your macro Best_Excel_Tutorial was doing was to auto-fit the width of the column such that the typed text fit the single cell proportionately. By taking into consideration the above, you may think that the reason behind the piece of VBA code is to auto-fit the column in which the active cell is located in such a way that the text typed fits into a single column.

But if you are learning about Excel macros at the moment, you will be required to understand what each line of the code means. Therefore let's see the basics of VBA code.

Excel macro code fundamentals

In order to understand all the instructions behind the macro you have recorded, let's examine the entire piece of code line by line. We will then check it item wise because that is how Excel executes your macro. Don't worry if you do not understand all the lines below at the moment. The main purpose of this section is not to make the reader an expert in VBA but it is to provide a fundamental idea of how VBA works and more significantly to show you what instructions Excel will carry out to write the text line from the earlier chapter and color the active cell and also change the font color from red to blue.

You can notice while generating the macros that VBA code includes some actions which you did not carry out really. As per Walkenbach according to his book *Excel 2013 Bible*, this is just a by-product of the method used by Excel to translate the actions into code. In other words, there is no need to worry about the code lines which appear useless at the moment. They can be removed. The Programming Window which contains the code for the Excel macro you have developed has following parts,

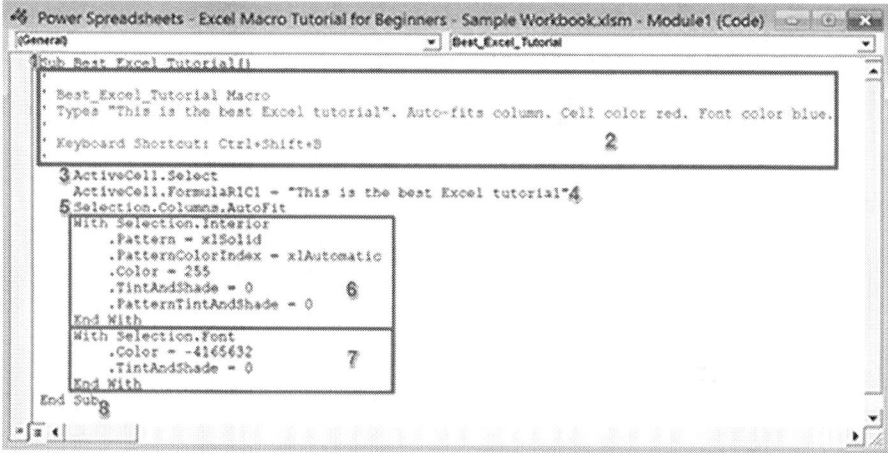

Item 1: Sub Best_Excel_Tutorial()

The term Sub stands for Sub Procedure. It is one of the 2 kinds of procedures you can use while developing Excel macros. The sub procedures carry out some activities or actions in Excel. The other kind of procedure is called as Function. The Function procedures are utilized to carry out some calculations and return a value. So what is the use of this line? It just informs Excel that you are writing a new Sub procedure. These procedures always need to begin with the word "Sub" followed by the name of the procedure and parentheses. Also, the Subs must end with "EndSub" as you may observe from the last line of the code. It is signaled by the number 8.

Item 2: VBA code lines in the green font

Here are the lines we are referring to,

' Best_Excel_Tutorial Macro

' Types "This is the best Excel tutorial". Auto-fits column. Cell color red. Font color blue.

' Keyboard Shortcut: Ctrl+Shift+B

These are just comments. The comments have these main characteristics,

- They start with an apostrophe or they are indicated by (').

- VBA fundamentally ignores all text that will come after the apostrophe all the way till the end of the line. So, when you are executing a macro, Excel will just ignore the comments.

- As a result of the previous action, the main reason for the existence of a comment is for displaying info regarding the specific macro and this will help you understand the macro. These comments can explain things such as the purpose of a procedure or the reason behind the recent modifications which are made by the procedure.

Item 3: ActiveCell.Select

As informed earlier, this line tells Excel to choose the currently active cell. More accurately,

- The ActiveCell refers to the current active cells in your active window.

- Select will activate an object on the currently active worksheet. In such a case, the currently active cell to whom the ActiveCell referred to.

Item 4: ActiveCell.FormulaR1C1 = "This is the best Excel tutorial"

The statement tells Excel to write "This is the best Excel tutorial" in its active cell. Now, let's check the individual portions of this line. You are already aware of the reason why ActiveCell is there. The FormulaR1C1 lets Excel know to set a formula for the object, in this case, it is the current active cells ActiveCell is referring to. It ends with R1C1 which is referring to the notation in which the cell reference is relative rather than absolute. Detailed explanation about the R1C1 can be found elsewhere. Remember, at the beginning of the chapter it was explained that you need to run a relative reference recording and how to actually do it. The text "This is the best Excel tutorial" states the formula. In this case, it is the text itself which needs to be placed in the object. The Object is the Active Cell in this case.

Item 5: Selection.Columns.AutoFit

As explained above, this statement forces Excel to auto-fit the column of its active cell so that its text which has the macro typed in it fits completely in it. Here are the reasons for the different portions of this statement,

Selection: It means the current selection which in this particular case is the active cell.

Columns: They select the columns of the selection and in this case, it is the column where the active cell gets located.

AutoFit: The word itself is self-explanatory. AutoFit sets the width of the chosen column like in this case or the height of the chosen rows to achieve the best possible fit.

Item 6: With…End With Statement 1

We are referring to the following set of lines that are known as With...End statement,

With Selection.Interior

    .Pattern = xlSolid

    .PatternColorIndex = xlAutomatic

    .Color = 255

    .TintAndShade = 0

    .PatternTintAndShade = 0

    End With

The macro you have created is already carrying out two of four actions it was developed to perform. Viz. it is typing "This is the best Excel tutorial" in the active cell and it is auto fitting the column width in order that the text that has been typed fits precisely. As you must have figured out, the next step Excel will take is to color the active cell with red. One might think that coloring the active cell is an easy step but, as it happens Excel must carry out many steps in order to carry out the action. This is the reason for the existence of With...End With statement.

The very purpose of the With...End With statement is to make the syntax simple with the execution of many instructions that refer to the exact same object every time. In the case of the example used in this chapter, this object is your active cell. As you may see from the screenshot provided below, the macro you have recorded has 2 With...End With statements.

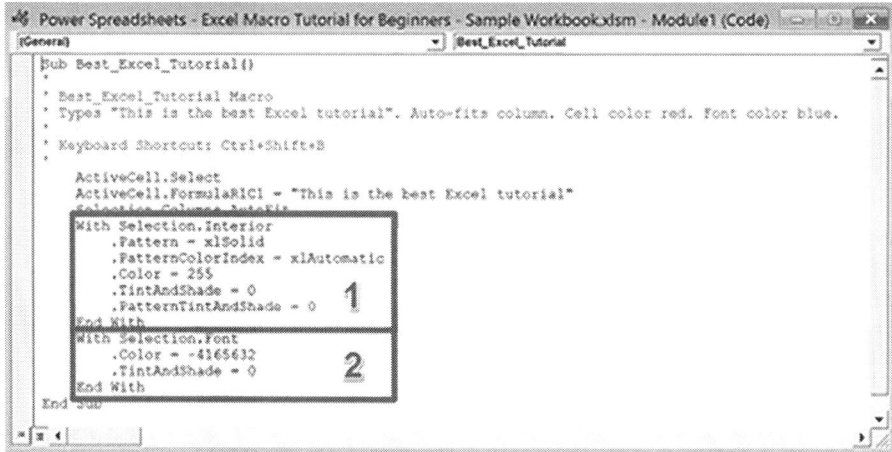

The With...End With statements come with the following structure. In the beginning, they have to state "With objectExpression". You can explore more about the meaning of "objectExpression". But for the moment it is sufficient to note that in the case of the example provided in the chapter, "objectExpression" is the "Selection. Interior" for the initial With...EndWith statement and "Selection.Font" for the next With...EndWith statement as explained below.

They might have one or some more lines code that are plain instructions which get executed on the object whose reference needs to be provided. In the end, it is said, "End With". For the first With...EndWith statement every object appears like follows,

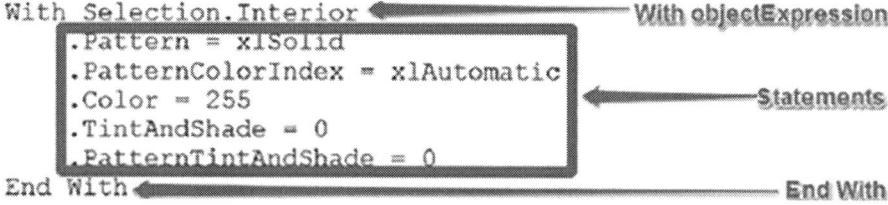

Now that the basic understanding of the With...End With statement is provided, we will go ahead and take a look at the initial lines one by one.

Line 1: The first line tells Excel that it needs to refer to the interior of the active cell while executing the statements which are a part of the With...End With statement. Now how to get this done? The beginning of the With...EndWith statement is "With" and it informs Excel that subsequent lines of code work with the object mentioned in the row. "Selection.Interior" is your "objectExpression" and it was explained while describing the structure of the With...EndWith statement. Selection means the current selection which in our case is the active cell and the "Interior" means the interior of the object which in our case is the interior of your active cell.

Line 2: Pattern = xlSolid.: This happens to be the first line of the With...EndWith statement and refers to the interior of your active cell. It instructs Excel to set the interior pattern of the active cell in order to avoid solid colors. This is achieved by doing this,

- "Pattern" will set the inner pattern.

- "xlSolid" will mark that the pattern needs to be of solid color.

Line 3: PatternColorIndex = xlAutomatic.: This line ensures automatic pattern for the inner of the active cell like this,

- "PatternColorIndex" will set the color for the inner pattern.

- "xlAutomatic" notes that this color needs to be an automatic one.

Line 4:.Color = 25.: This statement literally announces to Excel what color it is required to use for filling the interiors of the active cell. "Color" will assign the cell color but the number (in this case it is 25) clarifies the exact color which in the case of "Best_Excel_Tutorial" macro is red.

Line 5:.TintAndShade = 0.: The line instructs Excel to neither darken nor lighten the color which was chosen for filling the active cell. The "TintAndShade" will decide the darkening or lightening of the shade of the active cell color. When it is set to zero as in this case, this property gets fixed to neutral which means that there is no darkening or lightening of color chosen for the cell.

Line 6:.PatternTintAndShade = 0.: As can be seen from the wording, this line tells Excel that it should not either tint or shade the pattern for the active cell interiors. The .PatternTintAndShade will decide the tint and the shade pattern inside the object in this case and the chosen cell.

Line 7: End With.: The line conveys to Excel to end the With...EndWith statement. So, the subsequent lines of code will refer to the different objects that those to which the With...EndWith statement did. In the case of this example used in the chapter, the end of your first With...EndWith statement means that the subsequent statements are not referring to the active cell interiors.

Item 7: With...End With Statement 2 So far you have learned about the With EndWith statement and what its general structure is. So, let's straightaway get into the line-by-line explanation of the second With...EndWith statement included in the macro that as you may expect performs the last of the instructions that you provided while creating it. That is changing the font color of the cell in question to blue. You might be interested in knowing that the second With...EndWith statement is probably shorter than the first. Let us begin the line-by-line inspection,

Line 1: With Selection.Font.: As explained above, it is opening with a With...EndWith statement in which the With instructs Excel that the following statements will work with a certain object that appears here. The object in this case is Selection.Font. Now, what is Selection.Font.? Selection pertains to the current selection which for the Best_Excel_Tutorial macro happens to be the active cell and the "Font" refers to the font obviously. So in reality, Selection.Font indicates the font of the active cell text. So, "With Selection.Font" happens to be informing Excel that all lines of code which are a part of the With...EndWith statement is indeed referring to the active cell font.

Line 2:.Color = -4165632.: The line of code as you can expect from the line that indicates the intention much similar to the first With...EndWith statement above instructs Excel about the color which must be used for the active cell font. "Color" will assign a color wherein the number (in this case -4165632) is the color code that is blue in this case.

Line 3:.TintAndShade = 0.: The statement is really the same as the one from the lines included in the With...EndWith statement of above. It tells Excel to not darken or lighten the font color. As "TintAndShade" is responsible for either darkening or lightening of color while it equals to zero (as is the case here) Excel neither darkens nor lightens the font color of your active cell.

Line 4: End With.: This means the end of With...EndWith statement. So all the lines of code below this will not make any difference to the font of the active cells.

Item 8: EndSub: The End statement terminates the execution of certain things which in this case is a Sub procedure. This indicates that once Excel is finished executing this line of code, the macro you would have created will stop running. In other words, it is the end of the code of the macro.

Some Final tips for Learning Macros

If you are ready to go that extra mile for the purpose of speeding up the learning process of Excel Macros, here are some tips that will help you out. You can try them with the example given in the chapter. Keep the example Workbook ready for a further improvement in your knowledge.

Tip 1: **Make changes to the different parts of VBA code for trying new things**: For instance, change "ActiveCell.FormulaR1C1 = "This is the best Excel tutorial"" to "ActiveCell.FormulaR1C1 = "I love Microsoft Excel"", and see the results to check whether it has worked or not.

You may also change the number that indicates the cell filling and its font color. For instance, change from "Color=255 to "Color=10" and also "Color=-4165632" to "Color=200".

Tip 2: Delete some statement from VBA code to check how it affects the macro: For instance, what do you say will happen if you delete the "Selection.Columns.AutoFit"?

You may also change the number that indicates the cell filling and its font color. For instance, change from "Color=255 to "Color=10" and also "Color=-4165632" to "Color=200".

Go back to your main Excel window to run the macro again by using the keyboard shortcut like "Ctrl+Shift+B" which was assigned by you and check what happens. Results you have obtained have changed a great deal, haven't they? It is interesting to note how a couple of minor changes in VBA code can result in major differences in output.

Tip 3: Repeat the exercises included in this book: One of the easiest and best ways of learning Excel macro codes is by repeating the exercises added in this book. We encourage you to follow them. Record Excel macros which are different from those that appear in this book for beginners. Try out new things to check what happens. For example, open the VBE and go through the code line by line in order to understand the purpose of every statement. What is even better is that if you have a large enough screen or have two monitors, you can set up the screen in such a manner that you can observe the code that is generated in the VB Editor windows.

Tip 4: Read a lot and study: For example, you can read the authentic resources available online in order to find Excel tutorials about macros and VBA. In addition, register to these sites for receiving newsletters by providing them with your email id. That will ensure that you do not miss out on any future posts and updates.

Chapter 6

Ways of Optimizing
VBA Code for faster macros

Now, let's have a chapter for improving your knowledge and learn about the good practices followed by and used effectively by VBA programmers. These will put you in the same league as the high-quality VBA programmers. VBA programs are popular because they save time and this chapter will tell you about saving more time by using them. Read the methods carefully and see new pathways of innovation opened for creating Excel reports, dashboards, and automation.

1. **Analyzing the logic**: Before optimization of the syntax, please pay more attention to the optimization of logic. Without proper logic, the well written VBA macros programs will have no value. Therefore streamline the program logic and achieve the best performance out of the macros.

2. **Turn off the screen updating**: Avoid screen flickering or screen repainting by using,

Application.ScreenUpdating = False 'For turning off at the beginning of a code.

Application.ScreenUpdating = False 'For turning on at the ending of the code.

3. **Turn off the automatic calculations**: Whenever the content of an active cell or a number of cells is changed, the various formulae dependent on the cell change and so do the volatile functions which get

recalculated. Fortunately, you can turn off the automatic calculations by using,

Application.Calculation = xlCalculationManual 'For turning off the automatic calculation.

Application.Calculation = xlCalculationAutomatic 'For turning on the automatic calculation.

Now when you are required to calculate the formulae by using the program logic (this is because the macros depend on existing formulae), you will be required to use the following code,

ActiveSheet.Calculate ' For calculating the formulas of Active Worksheet.

Application. Calculate ' For calculating the formulas of the active workbook or all the workbooks in the current application.

4. **Disable the Events**: Stop the events by using Application.EnableEvents. You can tell VBA processor about firing the events. The events are rarely fired for every cell being changed with the code. Therefore, turning off the events will quicken up VBA code performance.

5. **Hide the Page Breaks**: When you are running MS VBA macros in the latest versions of MS Excel, the macros will take longer to complete than normal. They will take a longer time than even the earlier versions of Excel. For instance, a macro which requires many seconds to complete in the earlier versions of Excel will need several minutes to complete in the latest Excel versions. This issue occurs when some of the conditions are true. The solution is to disable the page breaks by using ActiveSheet.DisplayPageBreaks = False. For more information, refer to this Microsoft article: http://support.microsoft.com/kb/199505.

6. **Using "With" Statement while working with objects**: When we are trying to access the properties and methods of an object in several lines, we need to avoid using the object name or the fully qualified object path

repeatedly. It is irritating for VBA processor as it has to fully qualify those objects every time. Isn't it annoying for anyone when some task or work is instructed to us again and again? Yes, that's the case!

SLOW MACRO	FAST MACRO

Sheets(1).Range("A1:E1").Font.Italic = True
 	
Sheets(1).Range("A1:E1").Font.Interior.Color = vbRed
 	
Sheets(1).Range("A1:E1").MergeCells = True
	With Sheets(1).Range("A1:E1")
	    .Font.Italic = True
	    .Font.Interior.Color = vbRed
	    .MergeCells = True
	
	End With

The significance to be remembered here is that the minimum qualifying for an object by a VBA processor that is using minimum dots or periods (.) in the code. The concept lets us use A1 instead of Range ("A1") and Range ("StockRange")(3,4) instead of Range("StockRange").Cells(3,4).

7. **Use vbNullString rather than ""(two double quotes)**: The vbNullString is slightly quicker than the double quotes as the vbNullString is not a string in reality but a constant set with 0 bytes. On the other hand, the double quotes are one string that consumes at least 4 to 6 bytes for its existence. For instance rather than strVariable = "", you can use strVariable = vbNullString.

8. **Release the memory used by object variables**: When we create an object in VBA we are in reality creating two things, an object and a pointer which is also referred to an object reference. We may say, "VB does not use pointers" however it is not true. VB does not allow you to manage the pointers happens to be a more accurate statement. Behind the scene, VB regularly makes use of pointers. In order to destroy some object in VB, you can set it as Nothing but hang on a minute. If we are always using object pointers how can we set this object as Nothing? Well, the answer is we can't. When we are setting the reference to

55

Nothing there is something called the garbage collector which creeps up. The little piece of software makes the decision whether the object needs to be destroyed. There are several ways to employ this garbage collector but the VB makes use of a way called as a reference count method.

Once the VB has interpreted the last line where the object is generally set to Nothing, it will move the existing reference. At the point of time, the object will have no more references. The garbage collector would destroy the object will empty all its resources. If any other references point to the exact same object, this object will not get destroyed.

9. **Decrease the number of lines by using a colon (:)**: You may avoid multiple statements typically when it is possible to club them together in a single line. For instance, see these two macros,

SLOW MACRO	FAST MACRO

With Selection
  .WrapText = True
  .ShrinkToFit = False
 	
End With
	With Selection
	  .WrapText = True:
	.ShrinkToFit = False
	
	End With

As can be seen from above, multiple statements can be clubbed into one by using the colon character (:). Once you do this by using multiple statements, it reduces the readability at the same time increases the speed though.

The logic used by the Compiler: When we are saving a macro, it gets virtually compiled and unlike the human-readable form similar to the one we find in Visual Basic Editor (VBE), keywords get saved as 3-byte tokens. Keywords are the dark blue words that cannot be used as variables. Also, they are faster to process as the computer understands them better. The comments, variables, and literal strings, on the other hand, are not keywords or directives and are saved "as is". VBA compiler tokenizes the word but not the lines and they do not get compressed with every line being maintained as it is and it ends with "Carriage Return".

Once VBA macro gets executed, the processor fetches a single line at a time. These tokens of the fetched lines get saved by virtual compilers. Then they are interpreted and executed and a next line is fetched. As we blend the multiple lines together by using a colon in a single line, we are reducing the number of fetch cycles VBA processor needs to go through.

The change will bring about small differences in time because of faster processors of the day. Also, you cannot have greater than 255 characters in a single line and you will not be able to debug the code efficiently by using F8. Therefore, it is sort of useless and there is no need to trade off readability for such a small change in time.

10. **Declare variables as Variable and constants as Constant**: Well, although it seems obvious, many of us do not follow this. For example,

Dim Pi As Double

Pi = 3.14159

Rather use,

Const Pi As Double

Pi = 3.14159

As this value never gets changed, it will get evaluated only once during the compilation, unlike the variables that get evaluated several times in the run time.

11. Avoid Copy Paste where it is not necessary: Follow the rules of this table,

Instead of	Use this:
Sheet1.Range("A1:A200").Copy Sheet2.Range("B1").PasteSpecial Application.CutCopyMode = False 'Clear Clipboard	'Bypass the Clipboard Sheet1.Range("A1:A200").Copy Destination:= Sheet2.Range("B1")
Sheet1.Range("A1:A200").Copy Sheet2.Range("B1").PasteSpecial xlPasteValues Application.CutCopyMode=False 'Clear Clipboard	'Bypass the Clipboard if only values are required Sheet2.Range("B1:B200").Value = Sheet1.Range("A1:A200").Value
Sheet1.Range("A1:A200").Copy Sheet2.Range("B1").PasteSpecial xlPasteFormulas Application.CutCopyMode=False 'Clear Clipboard	'Bypass the Clipboard if only formulas are required Sheet2.Range("B1:B200").Formula = Sheet1.Range("A1:A200").Formula 'Same can be done with FormulaR1C1 and Array Formulas.

12. Use the worksheet functions instead of developing your own logic: When we use Application.WorkSheetFunction, we are telling VBA processor to make use of native codes instead of interpreted codes as VBA understands the worksheet function better than the algorithms. Therefore, for instance, you can use,

```
mProduct =
Application.WorkSheetFunction.Product(Range("C5:C10"))
```

Instead of defining your own logic such as,

> mProduct = 1
>
> For i = 5 to 10
>
> mProduct = mProduct * Cells(3,i)
>
> Next

13. Use the statements "For Each" instead of "Indexed For": We may avoid using the Indexed For while looping through the collections. For instance, take the example of this code before this tip. This code can be slightly modified to,

> For Each myCell in Range("C5:C10")
>
> mProduct = mProduct * myCell.Value
>
> Next

It is in relation to the qualifying objects and similar to using the "With" statement.

14. Do not use "Macro Recorder" Like Code: This code will look great and will perform great eventually. You are better off catching it with an example. Therefore use,

> [A1].Interior.Color = vbRed
>
> Instead of
>
> Range("A1").Select
>
> Selection.Interior.Color = vbRed

The use of too much Select and Selection affects your performance drastically. You need to know why to go in a cell and later change the properties. Or instead why you wish to go to a pizza shop when you may enjoy the same at your home.

15. **Avoid using objects and variants in the declaration statement**: Think about some good logic and get rid of the variants and objects from the declaration statements. Viz. do not use Dim i As Variant or Dim mCell As Object. By attempting to be specific, we can save lots of system memory. This is useful particularly in the case of larger projects. We might not remember which entity has been declared as variant above and misuse the variable by assigning some value to it. It will get typecasted without errors. The variant descriptor is 16 bytes long and the double is 8 bytes long, long is 4 bytes in length and integer is 2 bytes long. Therefore use the Variant cautiously. For instance, use,

Dim i As Long rather than Dim i As Variant

In the same way,

> Dim mCell As Range 'or
>> Dim mSheet As Worksheet

Instead of,

>> Dim mCell As Object 'or
>> Dim mSheet As Object

16. **Declare the OLE objects directly**: Defining and declaring OLE objects in the declaration statement is called "Early Binding", however, defining and declaring an object is called Late Binding. It is better to prefer Early Binding over the Late Binding. For instance use,

Dim oXL As Excel.Application

Instead of,

> Dim oXL As Object
> Set oXL = CreateObject("Excel.Application")

Chapter 7

Shortcuts and Tips
for Excel VBA and Macros

Assigning keyboard shortcuts to macros

Let us see 2 different methods for creating keyboard shortcuts in order to run macros and also to learn the advantages and cons of both methods. Assigning the keyboard shortcuts to easy and complex macros will help you work faster in Excel. This is typically true when you are required to perform similar actions repeatedly. In the chapter, we will look at two popular methods to create the shortcut keys. The two ways are Macro Options window and Application.OnKey methods.

Method 1. The Macro Options Window: We can use Macro Options window in Excel for creating a shortcut key for calling macros. Here are the instructions for setting it up.

1. You can begin by moving to the Developer tab and then clicking the macros button. If you didn't see the Developer tab on the ribbon, you can use the instructions provided earlier in the book. Or you can use the keyboard shortcut Alt+F8 for this.

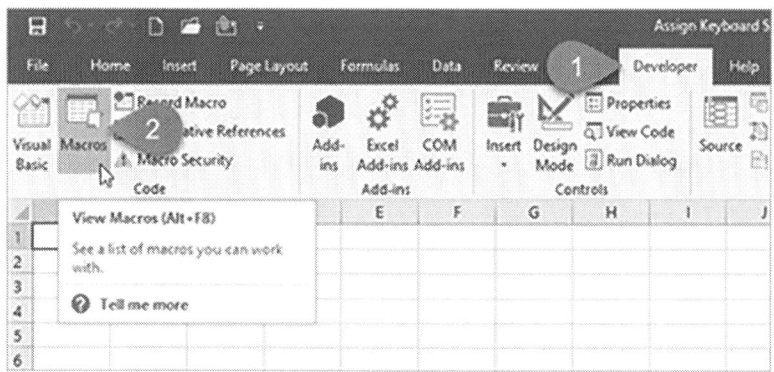

2. When you select the macro to which you want to assign the shortcut to, click on the Options button.

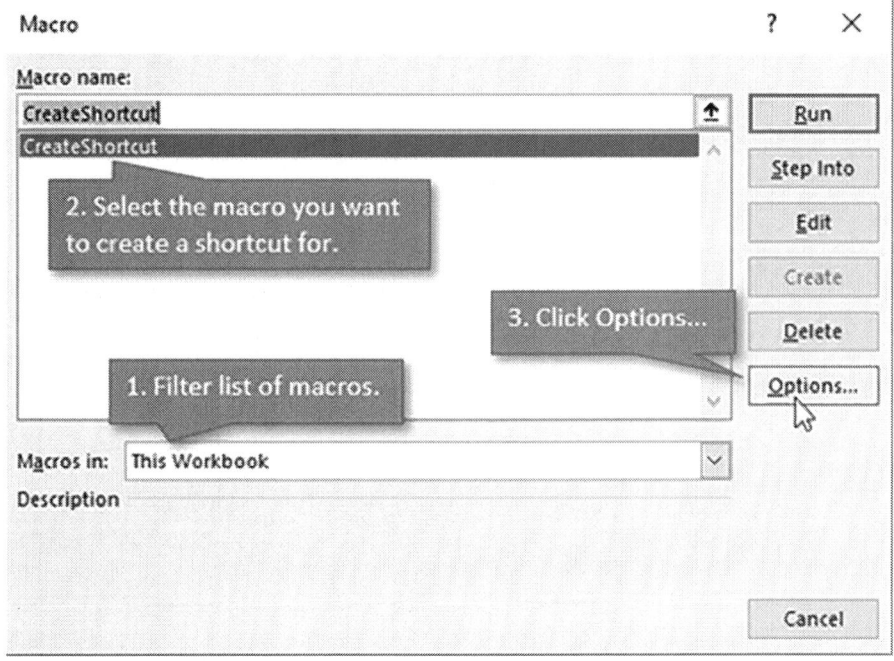

3. In the Macros Options Window, you need to create a shortcut you wish to add by adding a letter, symbol or number.

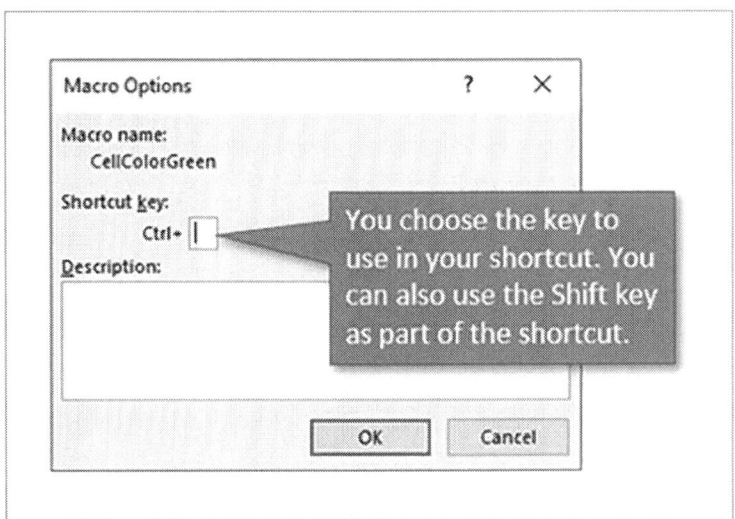

You must be careful that you don't override the existing shortcut which is used frequently like Ctrl+C for copying. One method for avoiding this is by adding Shift to the shortcut and make it more complex. In the example here, we are using Ctrl+Shift+C.

In order to delete a shortcut, just repeat the process of accessing the Macros Options Window and then deleting the characters you have entered for creating the shortcut.

Method 2: Application.OnKey Method of VBA:

VBA code can also be used to generate shortcut keys for macros. By using the Application.OnKey method we can create and remove the shortcuts. This also provides greater options and better flexibility for the keyboard shortcuts. You may start by using the VB Editor. You may do this by clicking the VB button of the Developer tab or by pressing Alt+F11 combination.

Create Shortcuts Using OnKey: In this method of the VB Editor, we will write some code for assigning the macros to keyboard shortcuts. First, create a new macro and appropriately name it as CreateShortcut or whatever name you wish for the procedure. Add a new line and then begin with a command Application.OnKey which will be followed by a space. Application.OnKey method has 2 parameters: one for the procedure and the other for the key. Key is the keyboard shortcut blend that is represented by key codes. A Procedure is the name of the macro which will be called when key combinations get pressed. Both these parameters are enclosed by quotation marks.

In the example given in this description "+^{C}" is used for the key parameter. + is a code for Ctrl, ^ is used for Shift and C is the key enclosed in braces. The complete list for the codes for every key can be found online. By following this code, you can name the procedure to which you are going to assign the key combination. In this particular case, we wish the key combination to run a macro called as "CellColorGreen".

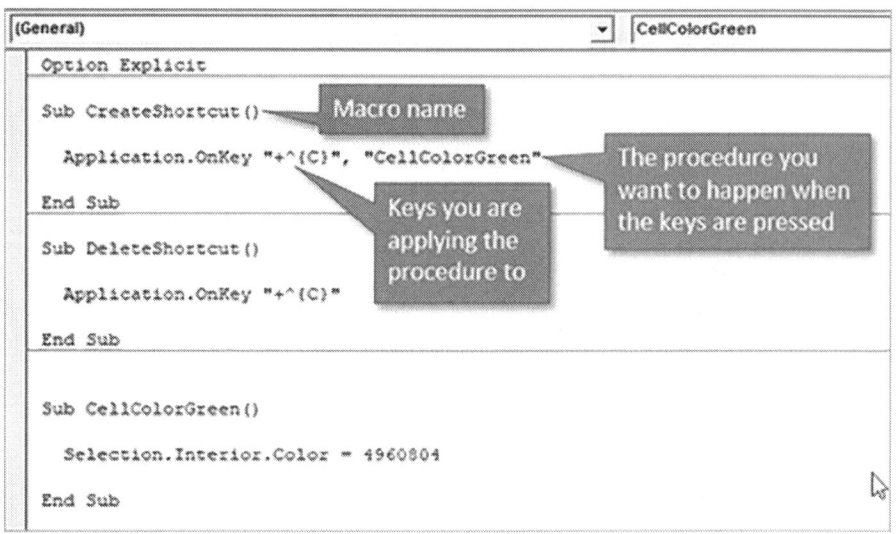

Delete shortcuts by using OnKey: This can be seen from the image above. The code used for deleting the process is quite simple. It is there just below the section that creates the shortcut. Rather than using "CreateShortcut" we will call it "DeleteShortcut" and we will remove the procedure name from the code. Absence of the procedure tells Excel to not assign actions to the keyboard strokes combination. It also resets the keyboard combinations to any of the native Excel keyboard shortcuts. For instance, if we are using Ctrl+C, the keyboard shortcut will revert back to doing the Copy action once the Ctrl+C gets pressed.

Create and Delete macros methods both will have many lines of code when using the OnKey method. It allows you to set up various shortcuts for different macros and all of that at the same time.

Automating the OnKey with Events:

You may actually automate this process by using the events Workbook_Open and Workbook_BeforeClose. Here are the instructions for setting this up,

1. In the Project Window of the VBE, double click on ThisWorkbook.

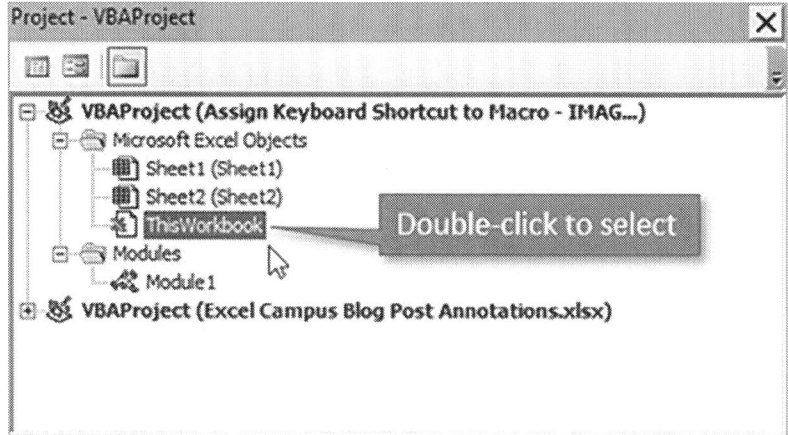

2. Select Workbook from the drop-down,

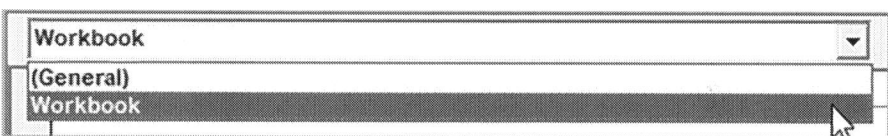

3. This will add the Workbook_Open event. Then add a line of code to call the macro you have created. In this case, the code will read as "Call Module1.CreateShortcut" without the quotes of course. You may also add an Event to delete this macro at any time you wish to close the workbook. Select BeforeClose from the drop-down on right and then call the macro.

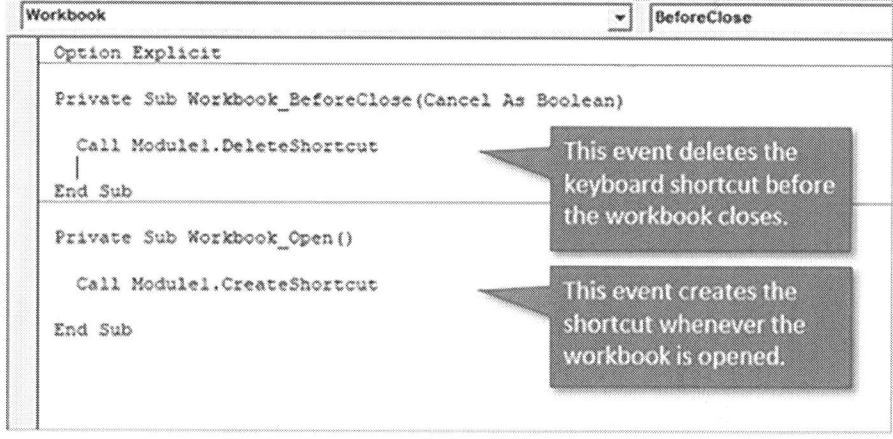

If the macros are stored in a personal macro workbook, you may follow the exact same procedure as above. You can find how to create personal macro workbook online and also learn about the advantages of having one.

Advantages and disadvantages of both methods

For both these methods, keyboard shortcuts can be utilized for every file we open in Excel as long as this file containing the macro will remain open. Let us look at some of the advantages and disadvantages of both methods.

Advantages of Macro Options Window:

Keyboard shortcuts are really easy to set up by using this method and they can be very appealing to the people who are worried about writing code.

Disadvantages of Macro Options Window:

1. There are limitations in terms of the keys which may be used for shortcuts. As there are limitations on using special keys such as Home, End, Page Up, etc.

2. Another problem can be that the user may have the same key already assigned, so as a developer if you assign some key for a workbook you cannot control which the user will run. It could be yours or his. The order in which it will run is alphabetic as the macro names of the open workbooks will appear on the user's machine.

3. There is no index available for the shortcut keys you have created and there is no way to even look for them. So if you have created many and can't remember, you will have trouble keeping track of the keys available. You will have macros which help in creating this list but it means additional work each time you wish to see the shortcuts.

Advantages of the Application.OnKey method

1. It is very easy to look up the keyboard shortcuts by searching VBA code for the word Onkey. You can use the find window (Ctrl+F) in the VBE.

2. If multiple workbooks or macros use the same shortcuts, you may control the priority or order of the running macros. Shortcuts that are created with the OnKey method supersede those developed using Macro Options window. Therefore, running the OnKey method will make sure that the macro referenced runs when the shortcut key is pressed.

3. It is easy to remove or delete the keyboard shortcuts. We may create macro buttons in the Ribbon for enabling or disabling the keyboard shortcuts. Alternatively, we may even use one keyboard shortcut to toggle the keyboard shortcuts.

4. You will be able to use some special keys apart from Ctrl, Shift, like Home, Alt, End, Page Down, etc. The combination of Alt+Ctrl provides several options for the shortcut keys.

5. The dynamic shortcuts will change the procedure which is called depending on the conditions in the workbook.

Disadvantages of Application.OnKey method

1. If there is a change in the name of a macro, your code will have to be updated.

2. You are actually needed to run the macros for assigning the shortcuts.

Conclusion

So which method is best suited for the macro shortcuts? Well, the Onkey method might win this race as it is a lot easier to find all shortcuts, have more key options, and better control over enabling and disabling multiple shortcuts. Although there isn't any perfect solution for this, it is recommended to use the Onkey method if you are going to use multiple shortcuts in your personal workbook.

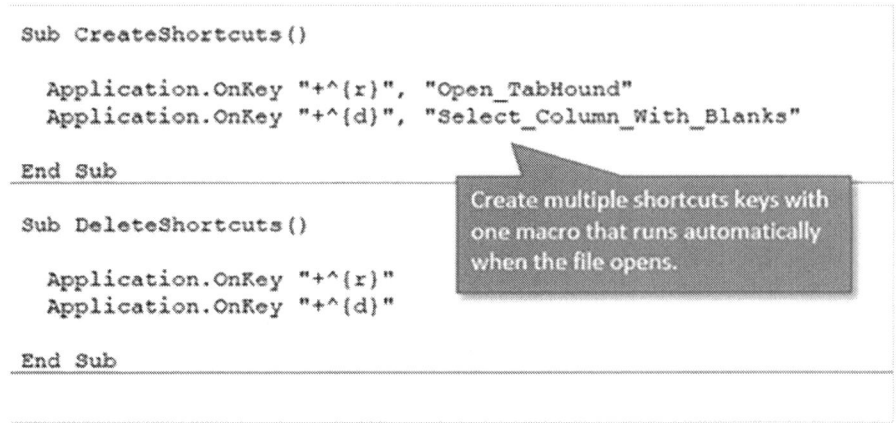

```
Sub CreateShortcuts()

  Application.OnKey "+^{r}", "Open_TabHound"
  Application.OnKey "+^{d}", "Select_Column_With_Blanks"

End Sub

Sub DeleteShortcuts()

  Application.OnKey "+^{r}"
  Application.OnKey "+^{d}"

End Sub
```

Create multiple shortcuts keys with one macro that runs automatically when the file opens.

18 Shortcuts for Excel VBA Macros

Here are some tips and shortcuts for saving time while writing VBA macros for Excel and other applications of Office. As we know there are a ton of tips and shortcuts available in VBA. But let's see some commonly needed ones,

1. **Alt+F11 for opening the VBE**: VBE or the VB Editor is an application we use for writing macros and for creating user forms. VBE can be opened by clicking the VB button available on the Developer tab in Excel.

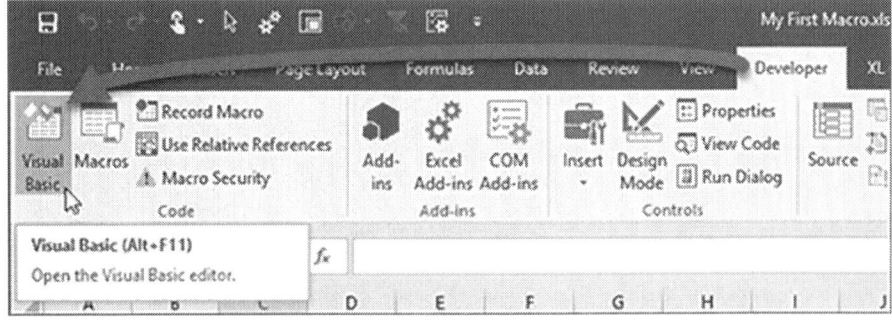

The keyboard shortcut used for opening the VBE in any Windows version of Excel is Alt+F11.

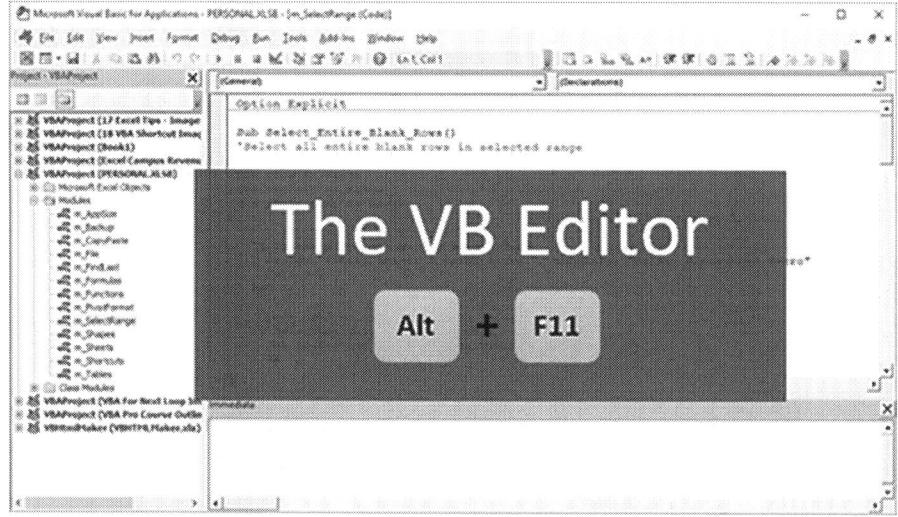

The same shortcut for the Mac version stands Opt+F11 or else Fn+Opt+F11. If you do not see the Developer tab in your Ribbon, click the image below to learn about enabling it.

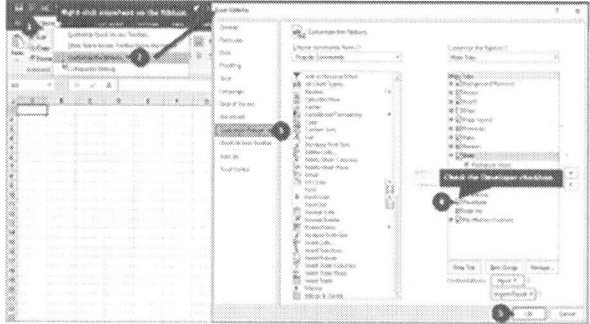

2. **Ctrl+Space for AutoComplete**: This is one of the most commonly used keyboard shortcuts in VBA by the developers. When you are using the codes, the Ctrl+Space opens an Intellisense dropdown menu which consists of a list of matching objects, methods, properties, variables and constants.

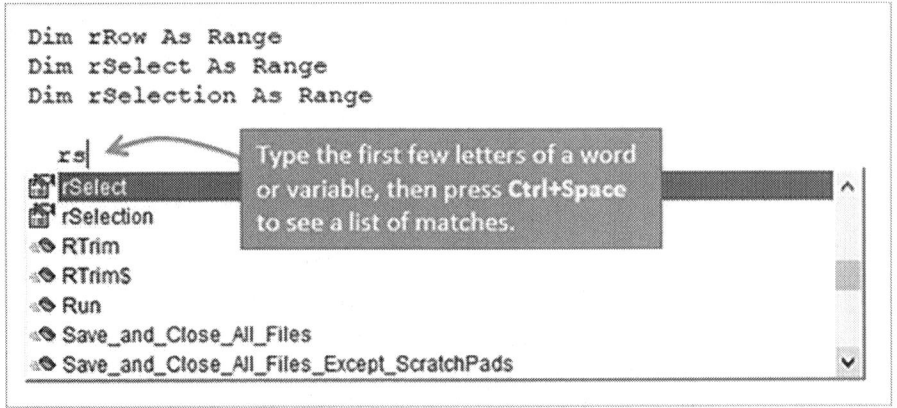

```
Dim rRow As Range
Dim rSelect As Range
Dim rSelection As Range

    rs|
rSelect
rSelection
RTrim
RTrim$
Run
Save_and_Close_All_Files
Save_and_Close_All_Files_Except_ScratchPads
```

Type the first few letters of a word or variable, then press **Ctrl+Space** to see a list of matches.

For using the Ctrl_Space shortcut in your VB Editor,

1. Begin to type a line of code such as ActiveCell.

2. After you have typed the first few letters, press Ctrl+Space.

3. You will find a list of all VBA words which begin with Act.

4. Press Up/Down arrows for selecting the word.

5. Now press Tab or Enter for completing the word.

There are 2 main advantages of the shortcut. These are massive time savers while debugging the codes.

1. It definitely saves the time involved in writing long words and also the variable names.

2. It stops the typos as VBA completes the words for you.

3. About the Function Keys on the Laptops: If you are using the laptop keyboard, you will be required to press and hold Fn key before you press the F11. The function key on the laptop is typically a multiple use key and needs the Fn key to be pressed for activating the function keys F1 to F12. Many laptops have an Fn lock feature which makes these function keys primary and it means that you will not have to press the Fn key while pressing F1-F12.

4. Intellisense for your Worksheets: We normally see the Intellisense dropdown menu when we type a period (.) in the VBE.

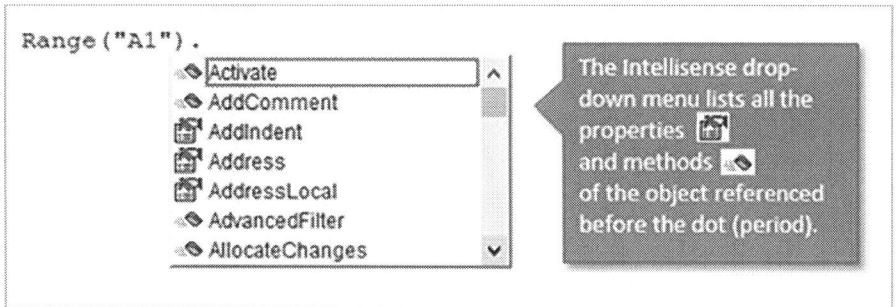

But it doesn't work many times. One of the common cases is the Worksheets property. If we press Worksheets("Sheet1"). We will not see the Intellisense menu. It can be frustrating and force you to think that maybe the Intellisense is not operational.

```
Worksheets("Sheet1").|
```
Where is the Intellisense drop down menu???

The reason behind it not working is that the Worksheets property contains references to one or more sheets. Depending on these references, properties and methods are different for every case. Actually, it would be great if the Intellisense would be intelligent enough to identify it however, it is one of those things everyone has to bear with. There are 2 ways of getting around it and see the Intellisense for the worksheets,

1. Use codename of the worksheets we are trying to reference. This is the easiest way of referencing the worksheets as the code will not break if the user is to change a sheet name.

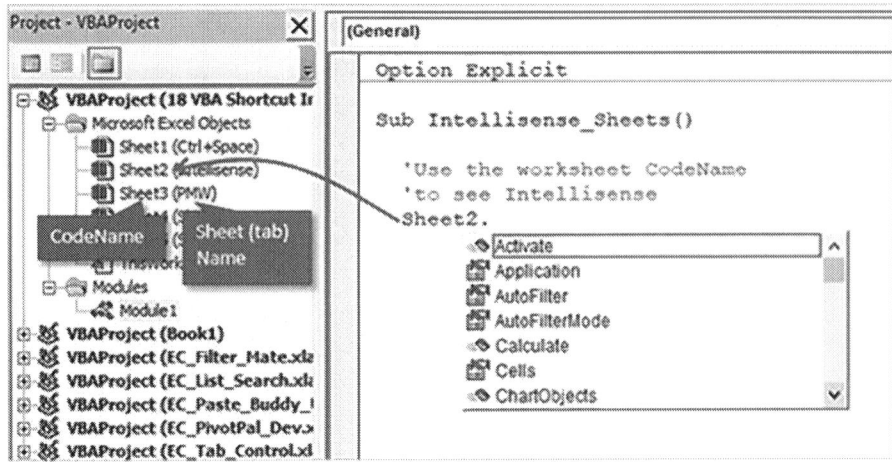

2. Set your worksheet onto a Worksheets object variable first. Now when we type variable name followed by a period (ws.) the Intellisense menu will surface.

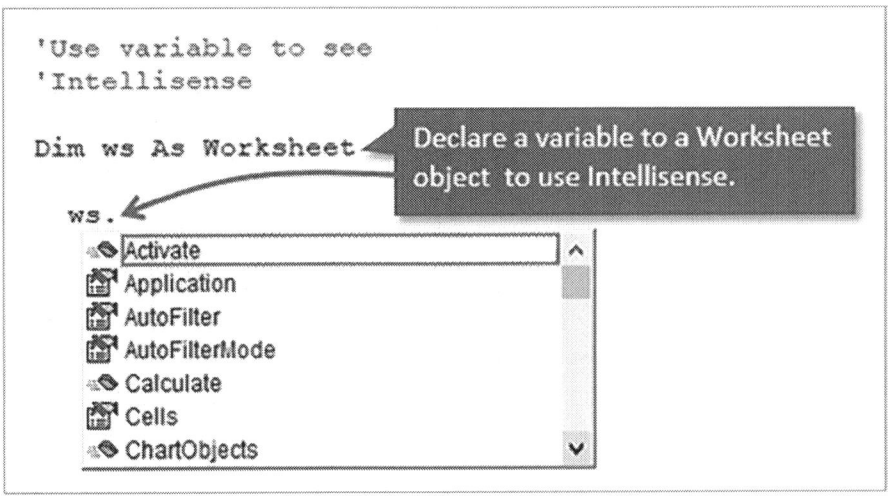

5. Liberal use of comments: We may add comments to the code which helps in explaining what every section of code will do. In order to create comments in VBA, you can press apostrophe at the start of a line and when you move the text cursor off the line, the text will turn green. This makes it easy to distinguish the comments while reading the code. VBA ignores the comment lines completely and you may add as many as you wish.

```
Sub Select_Column_With_Blanks()
    'Select all cells for the column of the activecell
    'in the current region of data (used cells)

    Dim lFirstRow As Long
    Dim lLastRow As Long
    Dim rActive As Range

    'Store reference of active cell to activate after selection
    Set rActive = ActiveCell

    'Exit if current region is a single cell
    If ActiveCell.CurrentRegion.Count = 1 Then Exit Sub

    'Find the last used cell in the column of the current region
    'Attempts to account for blank rows in the data by using Range.Find
    'to find the last used cell in the column of the current region.
    On Error Resume Next
        lLastRow = ActiveCell.CurrentRegion.EntireColumn.Find( _
                    What:="*", _
                    After:=ActiveCell.CurrentRegion.EntireColumn.Cells(1, 1), _
                    LookAt:=xlPart, _
                    LookIn:=xlFormulas, _
                    SearchOrder:=xlByRows, _
                    SearchDirection:=xlPrevious, _
                    MatchCase:=False).Row
    On Error GoTo 0

    'Find the first used row in the current region
    lFirstRow = ActiveCell.CurrentRegion.Row

    'Exit if any errors in setting the rows
    If lFirstRow = 0 Or lLastRow = 0 Then Exit Sub
```

Comment lines start with an apostrophe and have green text. They help describe what each line or section does, and make code easier to read.

Comment lines are **skipped** when the code runs.

However, commenting the code is a controversial topic of discussion. Many developers believe that precisely written code speaks for itself and there is no need to add any comments. Well, point taken but it might not work out for some people for these reasons,

1. When you come back to your projects some time later, you would have forgotten what the entire macro was doing. Comments are used as headings from a blog post. This makes it easy to scan through the macros and find the section you were looking for. These comments will also tell us what each section does quickly.

2. If you are sharing your VB project or hand it over to someone for maintenance, then it will be a lot easier to learn the code in the presence of lots of comments. It is like planning your legacy politely.

6. Use F8 to step through every line of code:

The keyboard shortcut used to step through every line of code is F8. In Mac it is Cmd+Shift+I. It allows us to test and debug every line of code in the macros. We may also open Excel side-by-side by using the VBE

73

or another separate monitor to visualize the actions performed in Excel as every line runs.

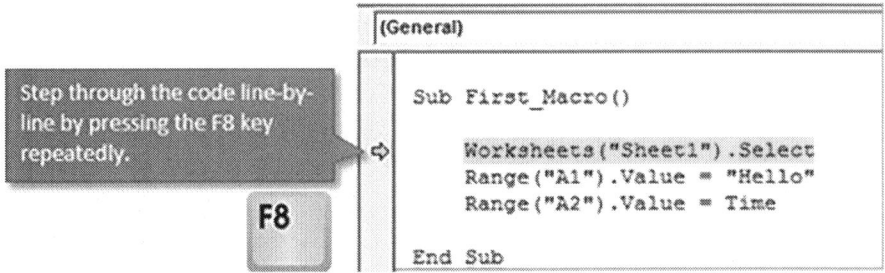

Many times this will help you find an error quickly with a reference to a sheet or a range. For using the Step into/Through shortcut,

1. Click inside the macro you need to run. You may click on any line of code there. This line will begin at the top.

2. Click F8.

3. The name of the macro will be highlighted in yellow.

4. Click F8 again for running the line and highlight your next line.

5. Keep on pressing F8 for running every line.

It is significant to note that the highlighted lines have not been run yet. The line will run only when you have pressed F8 again.

7. Assign Macros to the Shapes: Using sheet controls for buttons which run macros is a bit outdated in appearance. Luckily, we can also use shapes in Excel to run macros. These shapes can be colored or formatted in order to make them appear more like buttons you can find on the internet and mobile apps.

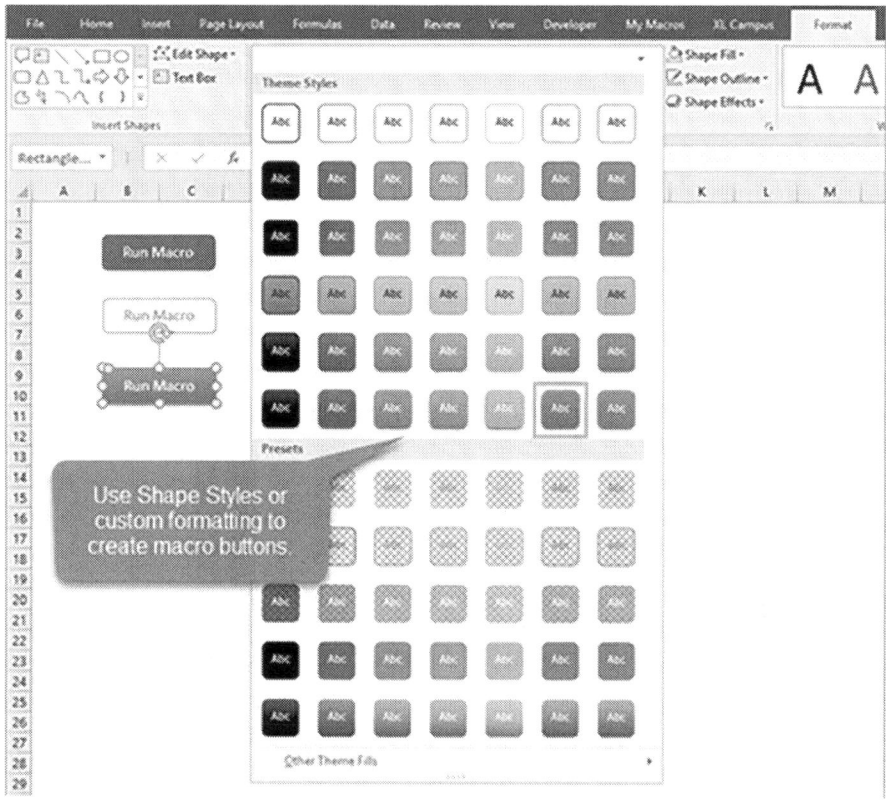

Assigning macros to a shape:

1. Insert one shape on your worksheet and format it the way you wish. This could normally be rectangular or circular and containing text.

2. Right click on the shape and select "Assign Macro.."

3. Choose the appropriate macro from the list and click OK. This macro will normally be the one which is stored in the same shape as your shape.

4. Click off the shape by choosing a cell from the worksheet.

5. When you hover on the shape, your cursor will switch to a hand pointer. Now clicking the shape will run the macro.

It is recommended to have a Yes/No message box appear just before the macro runs. It prevents any accidental presses of buttons.

8. Use the For Next loop for automating the repetitive tasks: There is always the requirement for performing repetitive tasks while using Excel. These tasks could be such as the application of formatting to multiple sheets, creating sheet lists, setting the filters on every pivot table, and copying data to every workbook, etc. Remember, loops are a very powerful tool in VBA and they allow you to automate certain tasks. It will loop through every item from a collection and perform whichever code you want on every item.

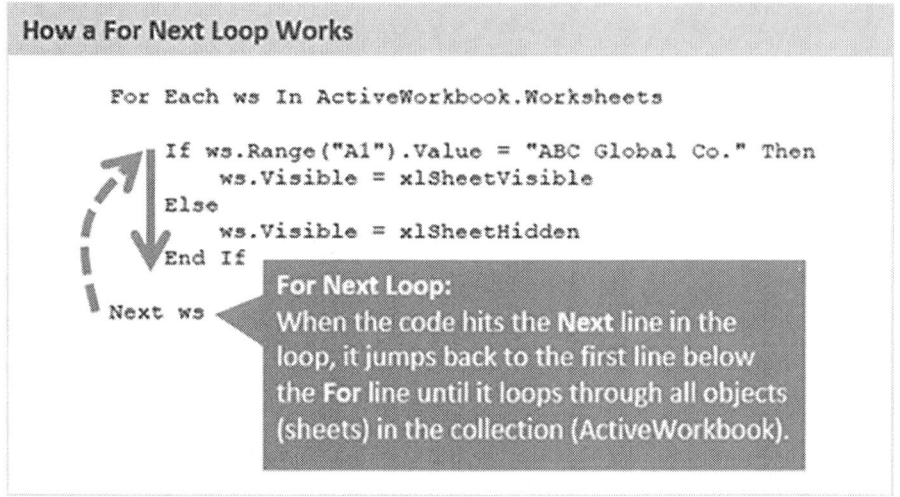

There are different kinds of loops but the For Next is the most commonly used. More detailed information about the loops can be found on the internet.

9. Using the Option Explicit: It is another controversial practice but it is recommended to use the Option Explicit for its benefits. Let's see why. It is needed here to declare all variables. When we observe lines of code having Dim statements on top of the macro, it is called declaring the variable. We have seen some examples of it in other chapters of the book.

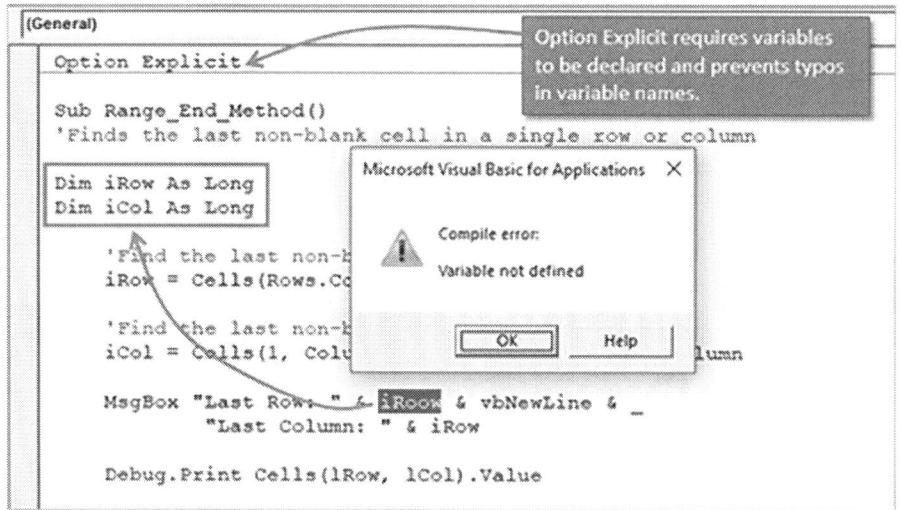

Here we are basically telling VBA to create a variable in its memory so that it can be used later when the code is running. We may, in that case, set values or references to the objects to the variables in your macro just below the Dim statement. The main benefit of the Option Explicit is that it prevents typos and as a result saves some time. If there is a typo and as a result, the variable is not declared, the VBE will throw a compiler error called Variable Not Defined. It will also highlight the variable so that you may declare it or fix the typo. When you do not have the Option Explicit ON and make the error of misspelling a variable, the code may still run but the results will show errors. If your macro is long, it will take a huge amount of time to find the typo. It is maddening so better to use the Option Explicit which will prevent these errors.

For turning ON the Option Explicit, you just need to type the words Option Explicit on top of the code module. You may get the VBE to automatically add the words to your new modules by going to Tools->Options->checking the "Require Variable Declaration" checkbox. The Option Explicit will appear at the top of every new code module you will create.

10. Using ListObjects (The Excel Tables): There are many benefits associated with using Excel tables in the workbooks. They can save some time by using auto-fill formulas, formatting data and they also work well as a source for the pivot tables. Excel tables make it simple to write VBA code for a range of dynamic data. It is a list or a data set in which the number of columns or rows keep on changing as you receive updated or new data. For instance, the following code refers to the cells between A2 and A15,

Range("A2:A10").Font.Bold = True

It is a hard-coded reference to the range. If you increase new data to its bottom, you will need to change the code manually for including new rows. But, if you store the data in Excel tables and refer the table column there is no need to worry about this.

	A	B	C	D	E	F
1	Date	Customer	Region	Product	Revenue	
2	01/05/15	Customer 4	West	Product 9	270	
3	03/12/15	Cust				
4	03/16/15	Cust				
5	03/27/15	Cust				
6	04/16/15	Cu				
7	04/16/15	Cust				
8	04/16/15	Customer 6	South	Product 3	70	
9	04/28/15	Customer 6	Midwest	Product 6	92	
10	07/06/15	Customer 6	Midwest	Product 7	128	
11						

Excel Tables (List Objects) make it easier to reference data that gets updated with new rows or columns.

Range ("Table1[Date]").Select

This following line of code refers to that same column,

Range("Table1[Date]").Font.Bold = True

The advantage, in this case, is that this code will automatically include newer rows added in the table. There is no need for manually updating or maintaining the code. We may also refer to Excel tables having ListObjects object, methods, and properties in VBA.

ActiveSheet.ListObjects("Table57").ListColumns("Date").Data BodyRange.Font.Bold = True

There are some definite advantages of using the ListObjects when you are modifying the table structure by adding or deleting the columns and rows, properties and are looping through the table.

11. Get the code using macro recorder: Macro recorder is a unique feature of VBA and Excel. As we take actions, it will create VBA code in Excel. For instance, once the macro recorder is turned on, you can go about doing your normal work in Excel such as copy-pasting data or writing formulas. Macro recorder will create all VBA code for the actions and will save it in the code module.

It is a great tool to use when you are first starting with macros and it also happens to be a great tool for learning and having snippets of the code. Excel object model is huge and it is impossible for anyone to memorize all the methods, properties and object references. Therefore, the macro recorder is a great method for getting some code for your pivot tables, slicers, list objects, shapes or any other objects you might be familiar with.

Although the macro recorder also has certain limitations. It will not create code for loops, error handling, if statements and message boxes, etc. We are required to write code for implementing these more advanced techniques which allow you to fully automate processes and develop applications in Excel.

12. Immediate Window: The Immediate Window of the VBE permits you to run single lines of code. You can run a method on an object or return the results of the code back to this Immediate Window. Suppose we wish to find out how many worksheets are there in a workbook,

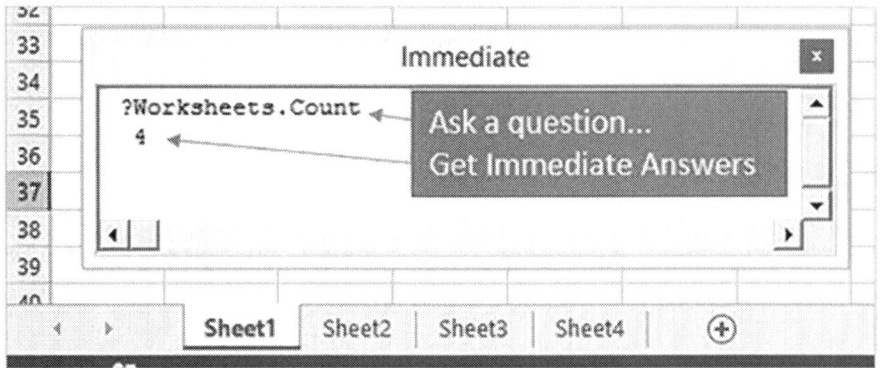

You can ask a question by typing say ?Worksheets.Count and hit the Enter button. The result of the query will be displayed in the next line. Immediate Window is also a place for the Debug.Print method outputs. The keyboard shortcut used to open the Immediate Window in VBE is Ctrl+G.

13. Assigning keyboard shortcuts for macros: This has been discussed in detail elsewhere in the book. But here is a recap anyway,

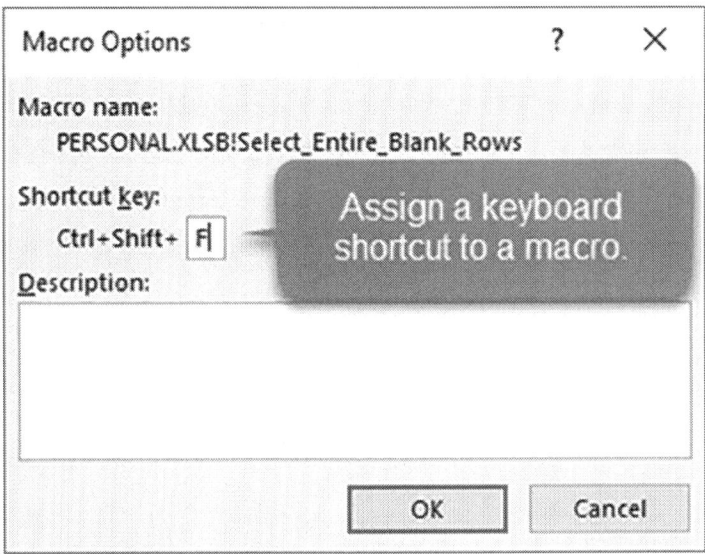

For assigning the keyboard shortcut, follow these steps,

1. Click the Macros button on the Developer tab or View tab inside the Ribbon.

2. Choose the file which contains the macro from the Macros In dropdown.

3. Choose the macro from your list box.

4. Click the "Options" button.

5. Type in the letter to which you wish to assign the macro to in the Shortcut key box. Remember all shortcuts begin with Ctrl. You may hold the Shift key when typing the letter for creating a Ctrl+Shift shortcut. It is normally recommended because most of these Ctrl+key combinations are previously allotted to other keyboard shortcuts in Excel.

6. Click OK and close your macros window.

7. Now you can press the shortcut key combinations for running the macros attached to them.

14. Checking whether a range is selected: Many times you might want to ensure that the user has a range of cells selected before the macro runs. If they have a shape such as charts, slicers, etc. chosen, then it may result in errors in the code. For instance, you may have a macro which deletes blank rows within the selected range. In order to have this macro run normally, the user must have a range of cells selected first. Here is the code which will verify whether a range is selected,

```
'Check that a range is selected

    If TypeName(Selection) <> "Range" Then

        MsgBox "Please select a range first.", vbOKOnly, "Select Range"

        Exit Sub

    End If
```

In it, the TypeName function will return data type or name of your object for given variables or objects. In this case, it will evaluate Selection and return type of objects that are selected. If it is not a range then the If statement will hold true. Typically this code is placed on top of the macro. If a range is not selected then message boxes or pop-up windows will appear which will instruct the user to choose a range. Exit Sub line will terminate the macro.

15. Ctrl+Y for deleting a line of code: By using the VBE, the Ctrl+Y you can delete a line of code indicated by the text cursor.

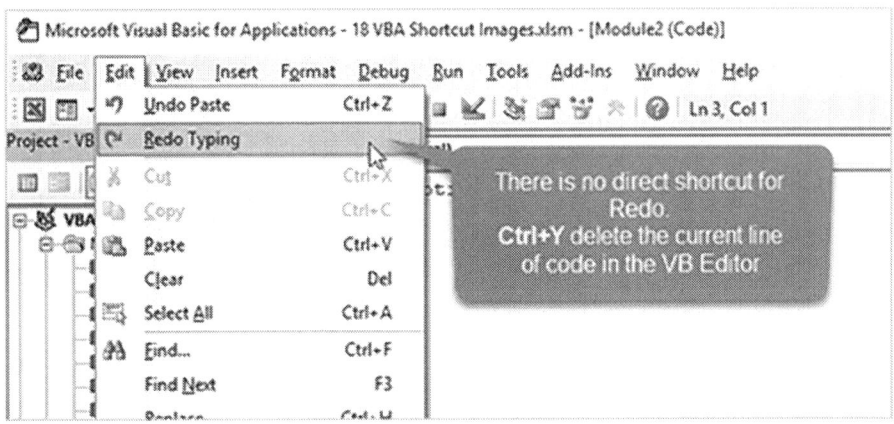

Actually, this creates some confusion as Ctrl+Y is normally used for the Redo command in just about all the other applications including Excel. If you look at the Edit menu from the VBE, you can see that there isn't a dedicated shortcut for the Redo. We may use Alt, R, or E as alternative shortcuts for the Redo. It is one of the strange parts of VBA and is good to understand.

16. Quick Info using Ctrl+i: It is another great keyboard shortcut to be aware of. Ctrl+i will display the screen tip which you can see while writing or running code. It permits you to see all the parameters of a property, function or method.

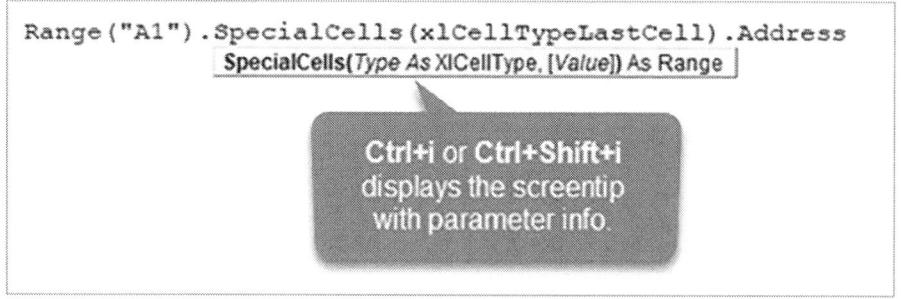

For using the Ctrl+i shortcut,

1. Place your text cursor on the word you wish to display info screen tip for.

2. Then press Ctrl+i.

3. Here the screen tip can be seen.

4. Press Escape for closing it or moving the cursor.

If you have a variable selected within the line and you wish to see the info of the parameters rather than the value of the variable or its data type then press Ctrl+Shift+i in order to see the parameter information.

17. Open Intellisense Drop down by using Ctrl+j: You can use the Ctrl+J shortcut for opening the Intellisense dropdown menu which displays a list of properties, objects, and methods, etc. It is common to use it when you have typed a partial line of code and have ended it with a period. For instance, Range(A1").

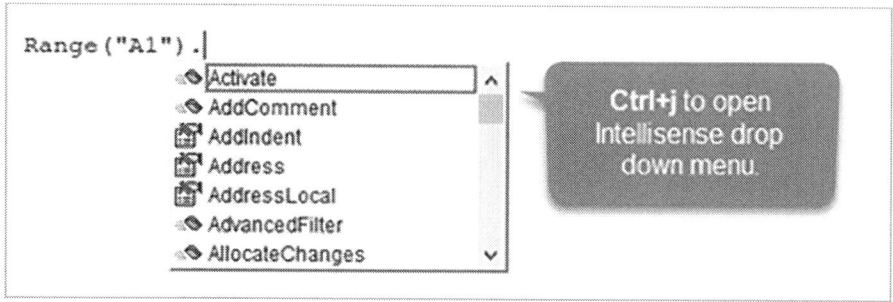

You can then come back to that line and see the Intellisense drop down. If you press Ctrl+J it will open the menu. Otherwise, you can delete the period and type again. You may also use Ctrl+J for selecting different variables from the list. If you have used wrong variable names anywhere or you need to change the name, press Ctrl+J for viewing the variable names list. If you prefix the variable names (for example as Hungarian notation) then other variables will be close by in the list.

18. Worksheet Functions: Are you aware that it is possible to use the worksheet functions in VBA? These functions are used in formulas in Excel such as match, vlookup, max, countif, max, min etc. Type WorksheetFunction., in the macro, to see the complete list of Excel functions which are available in VBA.

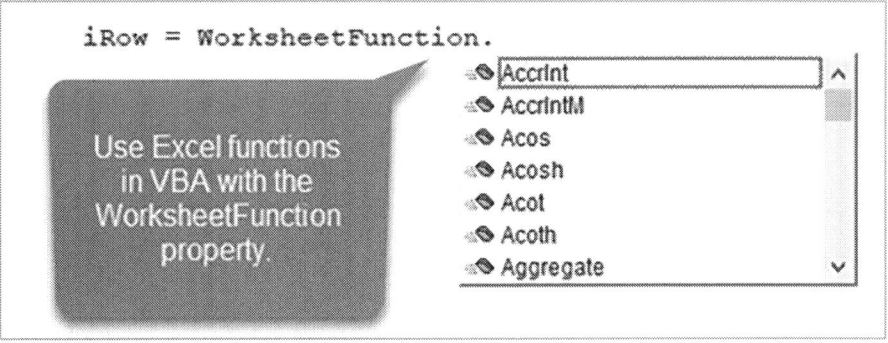

It is like achieving the best of both the worlds as we use the power of Excel functions with VBA code. The screen tip for the function indicates the number of arguments but does not display the names of these arguments. So we need to type the formula in Excel for determining what every argument is unless of course, you remember all of them.

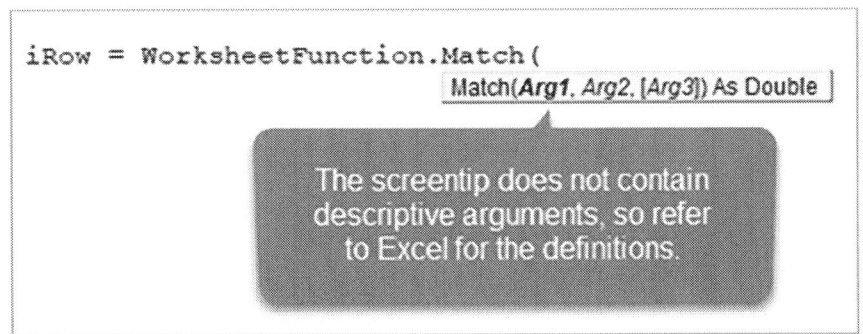

Although it varies with the person, the worksheet function most commonly used in VBA is Match. You can use the Match for looking up a value and returning the row or column number of that cell which contains its matching value. It might be easier than using the Range. Find method.

Chapter 8

Essential Terms for Learning Excel Macros and VBA Programming

Now that you have created your first Excel macro and learned about the various aspects regarding the creation of macros and the use of VBA programming, let's learn about the terms commonly used in macros and VBA programming. Remember, being able to create fundamental macros in Excel is just the start of a process of becoming an efficient and prolific user of VBA programming and macros. When you decide to unleash the power of the tools, you need to learn VBA. It is necessary because just recording a macro might not be enough for your requirements. The bad news is that using VBA requires you to understand programming. The good news is that Excel programming is not as difficult as it appears at first. Here are 16 essential terms you must know to learn VBA programming. You obviously need to know more but let's focus on the basic terms which you constantly find during the procedure to become a VBA expert. Some of these terms might sound strange to you at the moment but they will to most people not familiar with programming. VBA is a different language but it is not difficult to learn.

1. What is VBA?

VBA stands for Visual Basic for Applications. It is a programming language developed by Microsoft and it contains products that are a part of MS Office. This language comes with many functions but as the scope of this book is for the beginners, let's see the fundamental aspects of VBA. A programming language is like any other language you learn such as English, Spanish, Italian, Hindi, Korean, French, or Chinese. Language allows humans the capability to communicate anything they could imagine. Programming languages are a bit different as you are not using them to communicate with humans. You are using VBA, for example, to communicate with the computers. You are instructing the computer. So in other words, VBA is a language which allows you to communicate various instructions to MS Excel.

Therefore, there is no way around learning VBA if you wish to have the capability to automate tasks in Excel. VBA being a programming language is different from human languages and the codes you are using to communicate with the computers are different from those used to communicate with people. One of the main reasons for this is that despite the recent advances, the machines still cannot fully deal with human coding directly as it is. This is because they do not have eyes, ears, mouths, etc. for duplicating things in a certain way.

But, otherwise the programming languages are not significantly different, and so in order to learn VBA or similar languages, you must understand its structure. As this structure is not the same as human structure, you will encounter some terms you need to learn. You can make an analogy between the two in certain terms such as verbs, adverbs, and nouns in English with some components of VBA. For more information regarding how some parts of speech of normal human beings are comparable with some VBA components, you can consult *Excel 2013 VBA and Macros* a book written by Bill Jelen and Tracy Syrstad.

2. What is VBA code?

It might get a bit confusing from here onwards. Walkenbach explained in his book *Excel 2013 Bible* that you can perform actions in VBA by executing VBA code. There are two ways of generating VBA code. You can record some actions you are performing in an Excel workbook by using the macro recorder. Second method is writing VBA code in the

VB Editor. Here is a basic example of a VBA code. The comments are near the top in green and they explain what the code piece does.

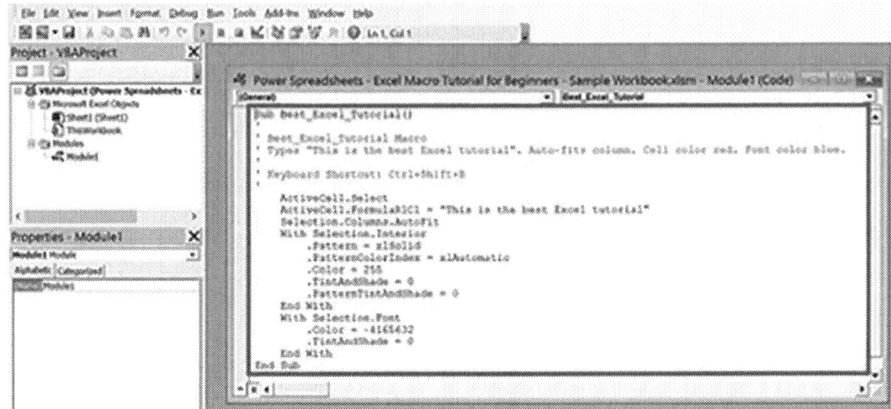

Now here is something about the difference between the macros and VBA code. Although it deviates from the purpose of the description, you can check out the exact description on various online forums. For the purpose of it now there is not much difference. As a matter of fact, MS explains that many programs that are a part of MS Office use this term macro for referring to VBA code.

Although, some distinguished Excel professionals and writers make a difference between macros and the code. For instance, while providing some key definitions in his book, Walkenbach differentiates between a code and a macro. Code is VBA instructions that get produced while recording the macro or while using it manually. And macro is a set of VBA instructions that are performed automatically. Now that these definitions of VBA, VBA codes and macros are established let's begin looking at the components of VBA.

3. Module

Speaking broadly, a module is the equivalent of a container for VBA. In other words, this is where Excel actually stores your VBA code. If you have seen a cargo port or ship or if you have been involved in shipping, you may have seen the intermodal containers like the ones that can be seen in the image below. The containers are used for storing goods among other things.

The equivalent of intermodal containers in Excel are modules and the equivalent of the goods stored in the modules are the pieces of VBA code. You may check which modules are stored in your Excel workbook that is currently in use in the Project Explorer. Project Explorer is a section of VBE (Visual Basic Editor). The following screenshots show an example of Project Explorer in which there is just the single standard module called Module1.

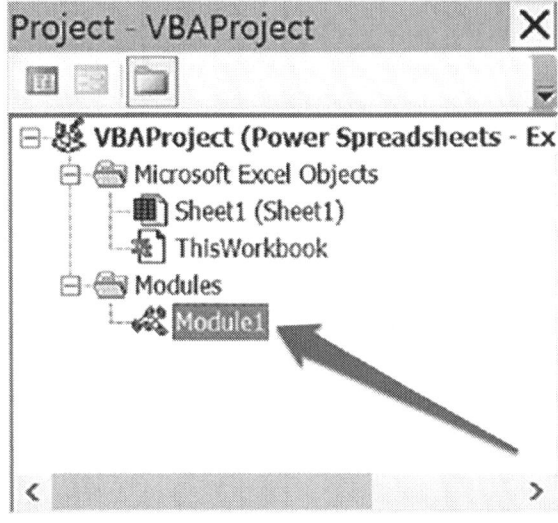

You can have other kinds of modules in addition to the standard modules however, the standard ones are simply referred to as modules. They are also made out of some procedures so the next term is the procedures.

4. Procedures and Routines

The procedure is a part of a computer program which performs a specific action or task. If you use technical terms, the procedure is a block of statements which is enclosed by a specific declaration statement having an End declaration. In his book called *Excel 2013 Power Programming with VBA*, the writer Walkenbach has explained how VBA supports two kinds of procedures. First is the Sub procedures that perform actions in Excel. The declaration statements that start the Sub procedure are called "Sub". For instance, the following VBA code piece is a sub procedure. You can see the comments near the top of the image which describe its purpose. See the opening declaration statement and the matching End declaration and also how this block of statements gets enclosed by the two declarations.

Functions are procedures that carry out the required calculation and return the result value. The Sub procedures do not return a value however, the function procedures may perform some activities before they return a value. The use of terms such as sub procedure, program, routine, macro and procedure can be a tiny bit confusing and they are used interchangeably in most cases. The most important difference is between a Sub and a Procedure as explained above.

5. Statement

Statements are instructions. In some of the contexts, you can distinguish between two main kinds of statements. First is the declaration statement which as indicated by the name, is used for declaring something such as a constant or a variable. While describing what a Sub procedure is, we saw the example of declaration statements. In this case however, the declaration statement happens to be the opening Sub statement that declares the Sub procedure called Best_Excel_Tutorial.

```
(General)                                              Best_Excel_Tutorial
Sub Best_Excel_Tutorial()
'
' Best_Excel_Tutorial Macro
' Types "This is the best Excel tutorial". Auto-fits column. Cell color red. Font color blue.
'
' Keyboard Shortcut: Ctrl+Shift+B
'
    ActiveCell.Select
    ActiveCell.FormulaR1C1 = "This is the best Excel tutorial"
    Selection.Columns.AutoFit
    With Selection.Interior
        .Pattern = xlSolid
        .PatternColorIndex = xlAutomatic
        .Color = 255
        .TintAndShade = 0
        .PatternTintAndShade = 0
    End With
    With Selection.Font
        .Color = -4165632
        .TintAndShade = 0
    End With
End Sub
```

The second type is the executable statement. These statements specify the exact action that needs to be taken. The macro Best_Excel_Tutorial which is used as an example above has many executable statements. For instance, the "Activecell.Select" statement instructs that Excel select the currently active cell.

```
(General)                                                      ▼  Best_Excel_Tutorial

Sub Best_Excel_Tutorial()
'
' Best_Excel_Tutorial Macro
' Types "This is the best Excel tutorial". Auto-fits column. Cell color red. Font color blue.
'
' Keyboard Shortcut: Ctrl+Shift+B
'
    ActiveCell.Select  ◄━━━━━━━━━━━━━━
    ActiveCell.FormulaR1C1 = "This is the best Excel tutorial"
    Selection.Columns.AutoFit
    With Selection.Interior
        .Pattern = xlSolid
        .PatternColorIndex = xlAutomatic
        .Color = 255
        .TintAndShade = 0
        .PatternTintAndShade = 0
    End With
    With Selection.Font
        .Color = -4165632
        .TintAndShade = 0
    End With
End Sub
```

There is a special kind of executable statement and it is called an assignment statement. This kind of statement as you may imagine from the name assigns a specific value or expression to a constant or variable.

6. Object

As we have seen above, the procedures perform actions or tasks. So what is the objective of these tasks? In other words, why is Excel performing this particular action? Well, the answer is Object. This is also where the analogy between VBA programming language parts and English speech parts comes in handy for understanding the logic of VBA and macros. So let's change the topic for some time and concentrate on English grammar. As stated by Grammar Girl in plain English, an Object is something that gets something done to it. In day-to-day life, you can find objects everywhere including examples such as a laptop which can be used for working on Excel.

Another example of objects are horses.

In VBA, things are not much different. This is so because as explained by Walkenbach in his book VBA Programming for Dummies, VBA manipulates the objects. As per Walkenbach, there are more than 100 classes of objects which can be manipulated by using VBA. Some examples of objects in VBA are workbooks, worksheets, cells, cell ranges, and cell fonts. Let's see if you can spot 2 objects in the Best_Excel_Tutorial macro which has been used as an example. If you can't do not worry, they will be pointed out in the upcoming screenshot.

```
(General)                                              Best_Excel_Tutorial
Sub Best_Excel_Tutorial()

' Best_Excel_Tutorial Macro
' Types "This is the best Excel tutorial". Auto-fits column. Cell color red. Font color blue.

' Keyboard Shortcut: Ctrl+Shift+B

    ActiveCell.Select
    ActiveCell.FormulaR1C1 = "This is the best Excel tutorial"
    Selection.Columns.AutoFit
    With Selection.Interior
        .Pattern = xlSolid
        .PatternColorIndex = xlAutomatic
        .Color = 255
        .TintAndShade = 0
        .PatternTintAndShade = 0
    End With
    With Selection.Font
        .Color = -4165632
        .TintAndShade = 0
    End With
End Sub
```

As explained by the prominent bloggers on the internet, the ActiveCell and Selection objects that are highlighted above are among the most commonly used objects. The ActiveCell refers to the currently active cell in your currently active Excel workbook. Selection pertains to currently selected objects that in the example illustrated above is the cell. The objects are defined by classes, therefore, the next query will be, what are classes? Let's see.

7. Classes

As mentioned above, the classes define objects and more specifically they define the following areas of the objects, such as properties, variables, events, and procedures. As a result of the above, you can consider the objects as examples of classes or similarly, you may consider them as blueprints. For instance, let's assume that you are running an organization that produces roll film cameras. This company had a basic technical drawing or blueprint like the one shown in the following illustration,

The blueprint defines characteristics of every roll film camera that is produced and therefore is the equivalent of VBA classes. When the organization has the blueprint, it can go on to produce the cameras.

The fully developed cameras are the equivalents of VBA objects. Classes are a more advanced Excel topic and as a result, you are thinking about working more with them in the beginning but just in case you wanted to know about them and how they are different from others and related to the objects.

8. Collections

In VBA, the term collection refers to the collection of objects. At the very fundamental level, the general use of word collection does not differ much from its use in VBA. As you may see in general terms, a collection of a group of objects or more precisely a group of related objects is called the Collection. So, the collections can be used to group and manage objects which are related internally. At the basic level, this concept of collections is pretty simple, however, if you wish for a more graphical illustration check out the collection for Dr. Seuss.

As described by Walkenbach in his book *Excel 2013 Power Programming with VBA,* the collection itself is an object although it belongs to the collection class. As the collections group the objects which have a common relationship between them, the next question is how are the objects related to one another.

9. Relationship of objects with each other

As explained by MS, the objects are related to each other in many ways but the main kind of relationship is that of containment. The containment relationships occur when the objects are placed within the container object. It means that the objects contain other objects in them like the plastic containers (which is one object) which hold the Dr. Seuss's books (they are other objects) from the image above. An example of the containment relationship is the collection of objects.

There is another significant kind of relationship which is hierarchical and is applicable to classes mostly. The hierarchical relationships happen when the class is derived from the more fundamental classes.

10. Property

Objects have properties such as attributes, qualities, and characteristics that can be used for describing an object. Walkenbach explains this in *Excel VBA Programming for Dummies*, VBA allows you to determine and change the properties of specific objects. Let's take the example of the horse,

What are his properties? They could be the color of his hair or his eyes or the size of his ears. In addition to having these properties, the objects also have methods so automatically the next question is, what are the methods?

11. Methods

For understanding the methods, let's go back to the example of English grammar. As explained above while defining the term "Object" it will have something done to it. A method is something that is done to an object. In other words, Walkenbach in the book VBA Programming for Dummies, the method is an action performed by Excel on the object. In English grammar terms and as explained by Bill Jelen and Tracy Syrstad in their book *Excel 2013 VBA and Macros*, the method in VBA is equivalent to a verb. Also, let's continue with the example of horses for explaining VBA components.

So, what is the example of a method or a verb which can be applied to a horse? What about horseback riding?

12. The appearance of properties and methods in Excel

Have a look at the Best_Excel_Tutorial macro being used for illustration in this chapter for the beginners. When you run the macro, Excel will do the following,

- It will type "This is the best Excel tutorial" in the active cell.

- Auto-fit the width of the column of your active cell.

- Colors your active cell to red.

- Change the color of the font of the active cell blue.

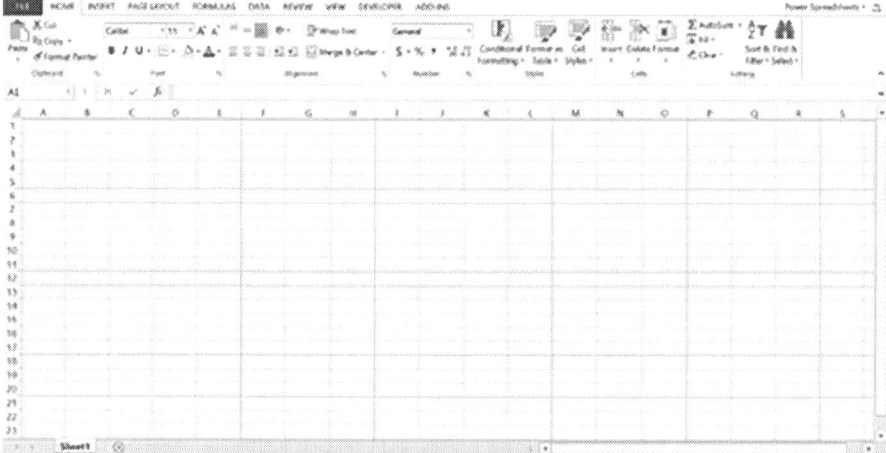

Now you are aware of what a property is and what a method is. Can you distinguish between them in the example illustrated above? For answering this question let's look at VBA code again.

```
Sub Best_Excel_Tutorial()
'
' Best_Excel_Tutorial Macro
' Types "This is the best Excel tutorial". Auto-fits column. Cell color red. Font color blue.
'
' Keyboard Shortcut: Ctrl+Shift+B
'
    ActiveCell.Select
    ActiveCell.FormulaR1C1 = "This is the best Excel tutorial"
    Selection.Columns.AutoFit
    With Selection.Interior
        .Pattern = xlSolid
        .PatternColorIndex = xlAutomatic
        .Color = 255
        .TintAndShade = 0
        .PatternTintAndShade = 0
    End With
    With Selection.Font
        .Color = -4165632
        .TintAndShade = 0
    End With
End Sub
```

Let us take an even closer look at the more relevant lines of code to decide whether it is referring to a property or a method. The line "ActiveCell.FormulaR1C1 = "This is the best Excel tutorial"" instructs Excel to write "This is the best Excel tutorial" in your active cell.

```
Sub Best_Excel_Tutorial()
'
' Best_Excel_Tutorial Macro
' Types "This is the best Excel tutorial". Auto-fits column. Cell color red. Font color blue.
'
' Keyboard Shortcut: Ctrl+Shift+B
'
    ActiveCell.Select
    ActiveCell.FormulaR1C1 = "This is the best Excel tutorial"
    Selection.Columns.AutoFit
    With Selection.Interior
        .Pattern = xlSolid
        .PatternColorIndex = xlAutomatic
        .Color = 255
        .TintAndShade = 0
        .PatternTintAndShade = 0
    End With
    With Selection.Font
        .Color = -4165632
        .TintAndShade = 0
    End With
End Sub
```

The ActiveCell will return an object. More precisely it will return the currently active cell. Now the question is, is the formula R1C1 a property or a method? It is property. More accurately the R1C1 sets the formula for ActiveCell. And the "Selection.Columns.AutoFit" tells Excel to auto-fit the active cell column,

```
Sub Best_Excel_Tutorial()
'
' Best_Excel_Tutorial Macro
' Types "This is the best Excel tutorial". Auto-fits column. Cell color red. Font color blue.
'
' Keyboard Shortcut: Ctrl+Shift+B
'
    ActiveCell.Select
    ActiveCell.FormulaR1C1 = "This is the best Excel tutorial"
    Selection.Columns.AutoFit
    With Selection.Interior
        .Pattern = xlSolid
        .PatternColorIndex = xlAutomatic
        .Color = 255
        .TintAndShade = 0
        .PatternTintAndShade = 0
    End With
    With Selection.Font
        .Color = -4165632
        .TintAndShade = 0
    End With
End Sub
```

In this case, your object gets represented by Selection.Columns which represents the column of the currently active cell. So, what is the balance part of the statement? Is the AutoFit a method or a property? If you said method, you are right. AutoFit is changing the width of the concerned column to get the best fit. In other words, it is doing something to the object (auto-fitting in this case).

The part of your first With EndWith statement which actually sets the color filling in the active cell is "Color=255".

```
Sub Best_Excel_Tutorial()
'
' Best_Excel_Tutorial Macro
' Types "This is the best Excel tutorial". Auto-fits column. Cell color red. Font color blue.
'
' Keyboard Shortcut: Ctrl+Shift+B
'
    ActiveCell.Select
    ActiveCell.FormulaR1C1 = "This is the best Excel tutorial"
    Selection.Columns.AutoFit
    With Selection.Interior
        .Pattern = xlSolid
        .PatternColorIndex = xlAutomatic
        .Color = 255
        .TintAndShade = 0
        .PatternTintAndShade = 0
    End With
    With Selection.Font
        .Color = -4165632
        .TintAndShade = 0
    End With
End Sub
```

All the independent statements in the With EndWith statement including the "Color=255" refer to the Selection. Interior. It is the interior part of the current selection and in this case, it is the active cell. So, the next question is, what is color, a property or a method? As color sets the main color of the interior of your active cell, your answer will be, property.

And finally the part of your second With EndWith statement which determines your font color will be ".Color = –4165632".

```
(General)                                              ▼  Best_Excel_Tutorial
Sub Best_Excel_Tutorial()
'
' Best_Excel_Tutorial Macro
' Types "This is the best Excel tutorial". Auto-fits column. Cell color red. Font color blue.
'
' Keyboard Shortcut: Ctrl+Shift+B
'
    ActiveCell.Select
    ActiveCell.FormulaR1C1 = "This is the best Excel tutorial"
    Selection.Columns.AutoFit
    With Selection.Interior
        .Pattern = xlSolid
        .PatternColorIndex = xlAutomatic
        .Color = 255
        .TintAndShade = 0
        .PatternTintAndShade = 0
    End With
    With Selection.Font
        .Color = -4165632
        .TintAndShade = 0
    End With
End Sub
```

This for all practical purposes is the same case as the above, especially for Excel beginners. In the case, a reference is made to Selection.Font which in this instance is the text font of the active cell. We have already seen that the color is a property.

13. Variables and Arrays

In the terminology of computer science, a variable is the storage location which you pair with a name and use it to represent a specific value. This value is stored in the machine memory. In other words, you make use of variables as placeholders for specific values. You should compare them with envelopes.

How do you use the envelopes for storing information? For instance, you can place some information in the envelope. This happens to be the envelope content or for the programming purpose, the value of the variable. Put a name on the envelope. This is the envelope name or variable. Now, let us think that you need to tell someone to get the info which is inside the envelope. You may describe the info that is required in these following ways. First is by describing the info itself. In such case, the person who is helping you must open each envelope to verify its contents. The second is by mentioning the names of the concerned envelopes. The person aiding you does not need to open every envelope to know where the piece of info that is needed is located.

Can you imagine why mentioning the name of the envelope rather than the information in it can be a more useful option? Let's get back to the example of horses. Let's say that you own one of the horses shown in the image and a significant part of the horse's diet is the sugar cubes.

Suppose the horse has five different caretakers and every day he must eat between five to ten sugar cubes. In order to ensure that this takes place, you will set the following rule. Every caretaker must give one or two sugar cubes daily to the horses. At the start of every day, all the caretakers must report to the manager exactly how many sugar cubes he provided to the horse on the previous day. The report is replenished by using the following table of Excel.

Caretaker	No. of sugar cubes given to horse by Caretaker
1	
2	
3	
4	
5	

As you have an efficient manager, you can program a VBA application that will do this (let's call the application "Horse_Sugar_Cubes"). Ask every caretaker how many cubes he gave to the horse. If any of the caretakers have not followed the rule which requires him to provide one or two sugar cubes to the horse, the application will issue a reminder. Before taking a look at the VBA code for this, check out how the "Horse_Sugar_Cubes" macro will look like.

B	C	D	E	F	G	H	I	J
Caretaker	No. of sugar cubes given to horse by Caretaker							
1								
2								
3								
4								
5								

Before beginning the setup of your Horse_Sugar_Cubes app, you will want to use these two following variables. First variable for storing the quantity of sugar cubes given by a specific caretaker to the horse. You can call this variable as sugarCubes. The second variable will store the identification number of your caretaker. You can name this variable as caretakerNumber. Now how do you create the variables?

For creating the variables in VBA, you need to declare it. Once you have declared a variable, you will determine its name and the characteristics of a specific variable and tell the machine to allocate certain storage space. A variable can be declared in VBA by using a Dim statement. The variable declaration is explained in detail elsewhere in the book. For the moment, keep this in mind.

You can declare the variable at various levels. Where you declare the variable will determine when the variable is to be applied. For instance, you can declare a variable right at the top of the module. The variable called as module-level variable exists as long as the module is in a loaded condition. In addition, they are available for use in any procedures in the relevant modules.

You may also create variables having a limited reach by declaring them inside a procedure. In such a case, the variable will be known as a procedure-level variable. These variables can only be used within relevant procedures in which they have been declared. As you use variables for storing a different kind of data, define different types of variables. You may achieve this by using "As" keyword. Some of the types that you can specify for the variables are String, Boolean or Range. Here is how the variables caretakerNumber and sugarCubes can be declared in reality,

```
Dim caretakerNumber As Integer
Dim sugarCubes As Range
```

Now let's go back to the topic of variables and get deeper in the VBA Excel tutorial for the purpose of explaining how you can use the variables in Excel macros and help you keep track of the number of sugar cubes given to the horse every day. The variables which contain a single value are called as scalar variables. They are used while working on a single item. But what to do when you are working on a group of items which are related to each other? In such cases, you make use of arrays.

Arrays are nothing but a set of indexed elements which share the same data type and have logical relationships between them. This function is pretty much the same as a variable that holds values. The main point of difference between the two is that arrays can store multiple values while the scalar variables can store just a single value.

When you are using an array, you are referring to different elements of arrays that use common names and distinguish with numbers called index or subscript. For instance, if you had a group of ten horses that are numbered from 1 to 10, you may refer to them as horses (1), horses (2) and so on until you reach horses (10).

Let's move on with the study of main VBA components which appear in the Horse_Sugar_Cubes app by learning what a condition is.

14. Condition

A condition is an expression or a statement which evaluates to either true or false. After this depending on whether the statement has evaluated to be either true or false, Excel will execute (or not execute) a group of statements. As explained by David Malan who is a computer science professor at Harvard University, a condition is seen as something which needs to be true for something to happen. Can you imagine any ways of applying the conditional statements in VBA application you are developing for keeping track of the number of sugar cubes given to the horse by the caretakers? Remember, the conditional statement normally uses the If-Then structure.

If you have taken a close look at the description of two things the Horse_Sugar_Cubes app is supposed to do, you will notice that the second step follows the If-Then structure. More accurately, if if any of the caretakers do not follow regulations that need him to provide one or two cubes to the horse, then the Horse_Sugar_Cubes will provide a reminder.

If you are a regular Excel user, you would have noticed that the condition is not exclusive to VBA programming. For example, many Excel functions like the If function permits you to check whether the condition is true or false. And based on this result, it will do one thing or another. In addition to this, you may use other functions like IsNumber for performing logical tests.

There are many ways to structure the conditional statements in VBA. But for the purpose of Horse_Sugar_Cubes app, you may use If Then Else statement. How will it look inside the VBE? You can use the following code for If.. Then statement for your Horse_Sugar_Cubes application.

```
If sugarCubes.Value < 1 Or sugarCubes.Value > 2 Then
    MsgBox ("You should give 1 or 2 sugar cubes per day to the horse")
End If
```

Now, let's take a line-wise closer look at the code snippet. The initial line of the code states two conditions which can evaluate to true or false. This line asks Excel to check whether the value of SugarCubes is less than one or more than two. SugerCubes points to the number of sugar cubes a caretaker has given to the horse. In other words, this is where Excel will determine whether the caretaker has complied with the rule which needs him to give one or two sugar cubes every day to the horse.

If either of the conditions is true, Excel will execute the statement which appears in the second row. If neither of the two statements is true that if both are false, Excel will not execute the statement in the second row. The second line instructs Excel what to do if either of the conditions in the first line is true. If indeed the caretaker has not given any sugar cubes (meaning less than one) or has given more than two to the horse on the day, Excel will display a message in the dialogue box reminding that the caretaker should provide 1 or 2 cubes per day to the horse. The third line of code ends the If-Then-Else block.

Now, you are aware of how to create variables which store the quantity of sugar cubes provided to the horse by every caretaker and the id number of every caretaker. Now you are aware of the ways to get Excel to remind the caretakers about the regulations that stipulate one or two sugar cubes to the horse every day if they haven't done it.

You need one more VBA component to complete the fundamental structure of your Horse_Sugar_Cubes macro. How do you tell Excel to ask each and every caretaker how many cubes he handed out to the horse? The answer lies in the following section.

15. Loop

Loops are statements that are specified once however, get carried out many times. In other words, the loop is a specific statement which makes a group of instructions gets followed many times. Similar to the conditional statements, there are many ways to structure loops. But for the purpose of our application Horse_Sugar_Cubes, you may make use of ForEach-Next statement. This particular statement instructs Excel to execute a group of statements repeatedly for every component of a specific group. In reality, it works roughly as follows. This is for the Each_Next statement in the macro Horse_Sugar_Cubes which is used as an example in Excel VBA related chapter for beginners.

```
For Each sugarCubes In Range("C5:C9")
    sugarCubes.Value = InputBox("Number of sugar cubes given to horse by caretaker " & caretakerNumber)
    If sugarCubes.Value < 1 Or sugarCubes.Value > 2 Then
        MsgBox ("You should give 1 or 2 sugar cubes per day to the horse")
    End If
    caretakerNumber = caretakerNumber + 1
Next sugarCubes
```

Note the presence of the conditional statement explained above here.

```
For Each sugarCubes In Range("C5:C9")
    sugarCubes.Value = InputBox("Number of sugar cubes given to horse by caretaker " & caretakerNumber)
    If sugarCubes.Value < 1 Or sugarCubes.Value > 2 Then
        MsgBox ("You should give 1 or 2 sugar cubes per day to the horse")
    End If
    caretakerNumber = caretakerNumber + 1
Next sugarCubes
```

But what is relevant for the purpose of this chapter is the general structure of your ForEach-Next statement. Let's have a look at the structure. In the beginning a ForEach-Next statement will say, "For Each element of a certain kind in a specific group". If you consider the example above, this line is like this,

```
For Each sugarCubes In Range("C5:C9")
```

The word element here refers to the specific items in a collection through which the loop must run. In the example we are using, these elements are represented by sugarCubes. So in this particular case, the sugarCubes is defined as your Range object variable. If you are in a situation where the elements have not been declared previously, you can also declare its data type. The last part of the statement refers to a group in which these elements are present. In this case, it is the range of cells from C5 to C9. On this collection, the statements in the loop are repeated. In other words, Excel applies the set of instructions in the loop to the cells highlighted in the upcoming screenshot.

	A	B	C
1			
2			
3			
4		Caretaker	No. of sugar cubes given to horse by Caretaker
5		1	
6		2	
7		3	
8		4	
9		5	

The body of a ForEach-Next statement like the one in the Horse_Sugar_Cubes macro includes a number of instructions which Excel applied to every element in the group. This is as per what is stated in the first line. For the example we are using in this Excel macros book chapter for beginners, the body of statements will look as follows,

```
sugarCubes.Value = InputBox("Number of sugar cubes given to horse by caretaker " & caretakerNumber)
If sugarCubes.Value < 1 Or sugarCubes.Value > 2 Then
    MsgBox ("You should give 1 or 2 sugar cubes per day to the horse")
End If
caretakerNumber = caretakerNumber + 1
```

This group of statements stated above is a very fundamental example. We can have structures which are more complicated than this involving statements like ContinueFor or the ExitFor that can be used for transferring the control to the different parts of VBA code. The last statement in the ForEach-Next statement comes with the form "Next element". From the example, we are referring to it will look like this,

Next sugarCubes

The statement just terminates the definition of a loop and instructs Excel that after carrying out these instructions in the loop, move on to the next element. The next element, in this case, is sugarCubes.

To conclude, these opening and closing lines of the ForEach-Next statements tell Excel it must run the instructions which are inside a loop for every one of the five cells where the exact number of sugar cubes given to the horse by the caretakers is to be recorded.

Horse_Sugar_cubes! A macro example!

Before completing this macro Excel VBA chapter for beginners, let's take one final look at the full VBA code behind Horse_Sugar_Cubes macro for reviewing some essential terms which have been described in this chapter and understand every instruction behind the app.

For referencing how the Horse_Sugar_Cubes macro works look at the illustrations above. Now, let's go through the essential items of this macro and make some general comments about a further illustration of every item covered in the chapter.

1. General Aspects

This application called Horse_Sugar_cubes is written in VBA (Visual Basic for Applications). VBA is the programming language used to communicate the instructions to Excel. The application in itself is a macro which is a sequential instruction for Excel to follow. The codes which appear in the screenshots above are examples of VBA code. Some of the terms such as macros, Sub procedure, procedure, VBA code, and routine are used interchangeably at times. The VBA code used behind the application is saved by Excel inside a module which is the container which Excel uses for storing VBA code. This application Horse_Sugar_Cubes has many statements or instructions.

2. Sub Horse_Sugar_Cubes() and End Sub.

In the screenshot above, the first line of code declares a sub procedure called Horse_Sugar_cubes. The Sub procedure is a series of statements which are placed between the Sub and the End Sub statements. More precisely, the code is a part of a computer program which performs an action. Other main kinds of procedures in VBA are the function procedures that are used to carry out calculations and return specific values.

In the screenshot, we can see the last line of code which terminates the execution of your sub procedure Horse_Sugar_Cubes. Once Excel executes the line, your macro will stop running.

3. Dim sugarCubes as Range and Dim caretakerNumber As Integer

In VBA, the variables are normally declared by using Dim statements. After which, you may decide the name of the variable and its characteristics. Your machine will allocate a storage location to this variable and you may use your declared variable as your placeholder for a specific value. From the example above, we can see that two variables are declared. One is caretaker number which is an integer and the second is the sugarCubes which is declared as a Range.

4. caretakerNumber=1

This line of code is an assignment statement that assigns a value 1 to your variable caretakerNumber. Therefore as a consequence of this, each time the macro Horse_Sugar_Cubes is executed, the variable will be set to an initial value of 1.

114

5. For Each-Next Statement

```
(General)                                    Horse_Sugar_Cubes
Sub Horse_Sugar_Cubes()

' Horse_Sugar_Cubes Macro
' Keeps track of how many sugar cubes are given to the horse by each caretaker. If a caretaker doesn't give any cubes
' Keyboard Shortcut: Ctrl+Shift+R

    Dim caretakerNumber As Integer
    Dim sugarCubes As Range

    caretakerNumber = 1
    For Each sugarCubes In Range("C5:C9")
        sugarCubes.Value = InputBox("Number of sugar cubes given to horse by caretaker " & caretakerNumber)
        If sugarCubes.Value < 1 Or sugarCubes.Value > 2 Then
            MsgBox ("You should give 1 or 2 sugar cubes per day to the horse")
        End If
        caretakerNumber = caretakerNumber + 1
    Next sugarCubes

End Sub
```

The For Each-Next statement instructs Excel to execute a group of statements repeatedly for every member of a group. The kind of statement is one of the simplest methods of implementing a loop. It makes a specific group of instructions to be repeated many times. In the case of the application Horse_Sugar_Cubes macro, this loop instructs Excel to repeat a relevant set of instructions to every one of the five caretakers of your horse. Let's now look at the body of the statement For Each-Next for understanding the set of instructions which are repeated.

- sugarCubes.Value = InputBox("Number of sugar cubes given to horse by caretaker " & caretakerNumber).

```
(General)                                    Horse_Sugar_Cubes
Sub Horse_Sugar_Cubes()

' Horse_Sugar_Cubes Macro
' Keeps track of how many sugar cubes are given to the horse by each caretaker. If a caretaker doesn't give any cubes
' Keyboard Shortcut: Ctrl+Shift+R

    Dim caretakerNumber As Integer
    Dim sugarCubes As Range

    caretakerNumber = 1
    For Each sugarCubes In Range("C5:C9")
        sugarCubes.Value = InputBox("Number of sugar cubes given to horse by caretaker " & caretakerNumber)
        If sugarCubes.Value < 1 Or sugarCubes.Value > 2 Then
            MsgBox ("You should give 1 or 2 sugar cubes per day to the horse")
        End If
        caretakerNumber = caretakerNumber + 1
    Next sugarCubes

End Sub
```

The first portion of the line of code (sugarCubes.Value=) assigns a value to your variable sugarCubes. The second portion of the statement which is (InputBox("Number of sugar cubes given to horse by caretaker " & caretakerNumber)) asks Excel to display a pop-up input box which asks for the number of sugar cubes provided by the caretakers to the horse is entered. The number you input to the box gets recorded in the relevant cell of your Excel worksheet and it is the value that gets assigned to the sugarCubes variable.

Input box refers to every caretaker by his identification number (from one to five) by calling the caretakerNumber variable value (for instance the first caretaker is referenced by inputting caretaker 1 and so on). As a result of the statement immediately above the For Each-Next.statement (caretakerNumber=1), the variable value of caretakerNumber at the beginning of a process is always one. Let's see which statement asks Excel to update the variable caretakerNumber for its relevant caretaker.

Conditional statement

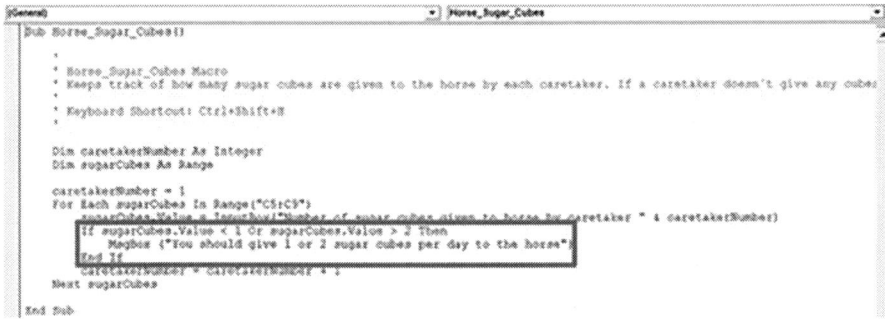

The conditional statement evaluates a specific condition and depending on the result whether it is true or false, Excel carries out or stops from carrying out some actions. The conditional statement used in Horse_Sugar_cubes macro evaluates if the caretaker has provided less than one or more than two sugar cubes to the horse. So not complying with the rule which needs them to provide either one or two sugar cubes daily to the horse. If any of the two conditions are met, Excel will display a message box having a reminder stating "You should give 1 or 2 sugar cubes per day to the horse".

caretakerNumber = caretakerNumber+1

The statement raises the value of a variable caretakerNumber by one for every successive repetition of the ForEach-Next statement. So, the second time this set of instructions gets repeated by Excel macro, the variable value equals to 2. Then the third time it is repeated it will have a value 3 and so on. As you might expect the fourth and fifth time the value will be 4 and 5.

Summary

So by now, you are aware of at least 16 necessary terms that are required for learning VBA programming. You can also tell how some of the terms are used interchangeably and we have carried out some discussions to clarify their applications. We have seen how these terms come together to create a macro and you know now that some of the terms used in the chapter can be used by the beginners in real practice.

Chapter 9

Interacting with Office Applications Using Excel and VBA

In this chapter, we will learn the following things,

1. Beginning or activating different applications from Excel.

2. Controlling the Office Word by using Excel and vice versa. Also sending personalized emails from Excel.

If you are familiar with using Excel, you must be aware of other applications that make the MS Office. Well, just about everyone makes use of MS Word and most people will be familiar with Access or PowerPoint. In the chapter, we will see some easy examples which demonstrate the use of Excel VBA for interacting with other MS Office applications.

Starting another Application from Excel

Starting other applications from Excel is useful quite often. For instance, you may wish to launch another MS Office application or even a DOS batch file while using Excel VBA macro.

Use VBA Shell Function

The VBA Shell function is useful in making the launching of another program easy. Here is an example of a code which starts a Windows Calculator program named CALC.EXE.

```
On Error Resume Next
AppActivate "Calculator"
If Err <> 0 Then
    Err = 0
    TaskID = Shell(Program, 1)
    If Err <> 0 Then MsgBox "Can't start " & Program
End If
End Sub
```

The modified procedure used here utilizes the AppActivate statement for activating the Windows Calculator application in this case if it is already running. The argument used for AppActivate is the Caption for the app's title bar. If the AppActivate statement develops an error, it indicates that the calculator is not running. When it is not running, the routine will start the application by using the Shell function.

Activating an MS Office Application

If the application that you wish to start is one of the many MS applications, you can use the ActivateMicrosoftApp method from the Application object. For instance, the following process can start Word.

```
Sub StartWord()
    Application.ActivateMicrosoftApp xlMicrosoftWord
End Sub
```

If Word is already running when this procedure gets executed, it will be activated. There are other constants available for the method,

xlMicrosoftPowerPoint (PowerPoint)

xlMicrosoftMail (Outlook)

xlMicrosoftAccess   (Access)   xlMicrosoftFoxPro   (FoxPro)
xlMicrosoftProject (Project) xlMicrosoftSchedulePlus (SchedulePlus)

Using Automation available in Excel

You may write a macro for controlling other applications like MS Word. More precisely, Excel macros control most significant components of

Word viz. the automation server. In these circumstances, Excel is referred to as the client application and Word is your server application.

```
Sub StartCalculator()
    Dim Program As String
    Dim TaskID As Double
    On Error Resume Next
    Program = "calc.exe"
    TaskID = Shell(Program, 1)
    If Err <> 0 Then
        MsgBox "Can't start " & Program
    End If
End Sub
```

The following screenshot shows a Windows Calculator which gets displayed as a result of running the procedure above.

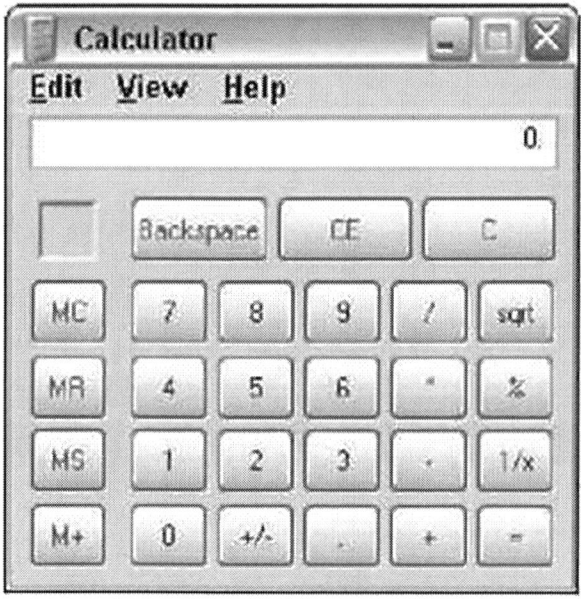

Program for Windows Calculator

Here, the Shell function will return a task identification number of the application. You may use the number later for activating the tasks. The second argument for the Shell function decides how the app will be displayed. 1 is the code for your normal sized window having focus. You may use the Help systems for other argument values.

If the Shell function is not successful, it will show an error. So, this procedure will use an OnError statement for displaying the appropriate message when the executable files cannot be found or if some other errors occur. However, the question is, what happens if the Calculator program is already running? The procedure StartCalculator just opens another instance of your program. In almost all cases, you will wish to activate the current instance. You can use the following slightly modified code for solving this problem.

```
Public TaskID

Sub StartCalculator2()
    Dim Program As String
    Dim TaskID As Double
    Program = "calc.exe"
```

The fundamental concept used behind automation is pretty appealing. The developer that needs to generate charts for example, can reach into another app's bag of objects. He can fetch a chart object and then modify its properties and make use of its methods. So the automation will burn the boundaries between various apps. For instance, using automation the end user may be working with Access objects in Excel and not even realizing it. Some applications like MS Excel can function either as client applications or server applications. Other applications function only as client applications or as server applications only. In the upcoming sections, we will see how VBA is used for accessing and manipulating objects that are exposed by other applications. These examples use MS Word however, the same concepts apply to other applications as well for exposing their objects for automation.

Getting the Version Number of your Word

The upcoming example shows how to create Word objects for providing access to different objects in the Word object model. The procedure will create an object, display the version number, close the Word application and then will destroy the object. This will free up the used memory.

```
Sub GetWordVersion()
    Dim WordApp As Object
    Set WordApp = CreateObject("Word.Application")
    MsgBox WordApp.Version
    WordApp.Quit
    Set WordApp = Nothing
End Sub
```

The Word object which is created in the procedure is invisible. If you wish to see the object when it is being manipulated, you can set its Visible property as True. This is done as follows,

WordApp.Visible = True

Most automation examples used in this chapter make use of late binding as opposed to the early one. So, what is the difference? While you are using early binding, you need to establish a reference to version specific object libraries by using the ToolsOReferences available in VBE (Visual Basic Editor). While you are using late binding, there is no need to set the reference although both approaches come with their share of pros and cons.

Control Word from Excel

The upcoming screenshot shows an automation session by using Word. The procedure MakeMemos used in the session creates 3 customized memos in Word and then stores every memo in a separate file. This information is used to create memos and is stored in a worksheet.

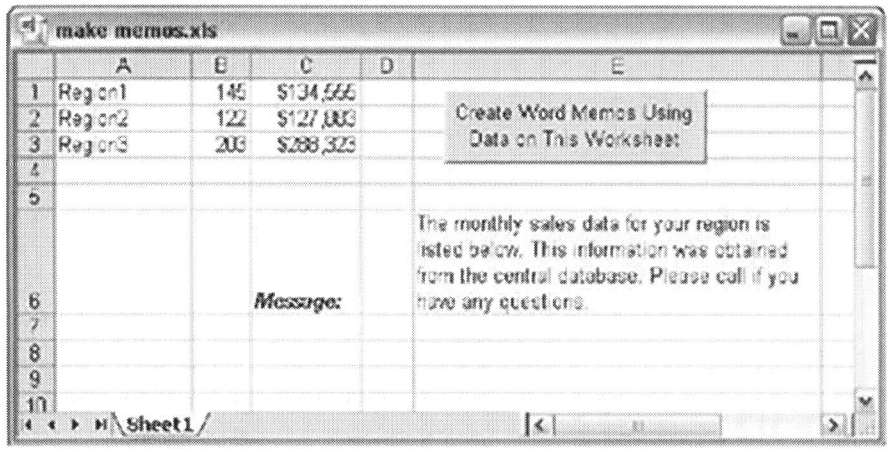

Word will automatically generate 3 memos based on the Excel data. The code used for the MakeMemos procedure is too long to be included here however, it can be found elsewhere on the internet, check it out. The MakeMemos procedure will begin by creating objects called WordApp. This routines goes through the 3 rows of data in the Sheet1 and makes use of Word properties and methods for creating every memo and save it to the drive. A range called Message in the cell E6 contains text used in the concerned memo. All this action takes place behind the scenes. Word will not be visible. The screenshot shows a document developed by the procedure MakeMemos.

Control Excel from Word

As you could have guessed, you may also control Excel from other applications such as another programming language or a Word VBA procedure. For instance, you may wish to perform certain calculations in Excel and return its results to the Word document. You can create all the following objects in Excel with adjacent functions.

Application object: CreateObject("Excel.Application")

Workbook object: CreateObject("Excel.Sheet")

Chart object: CreateObject("Excel.Chart")

123

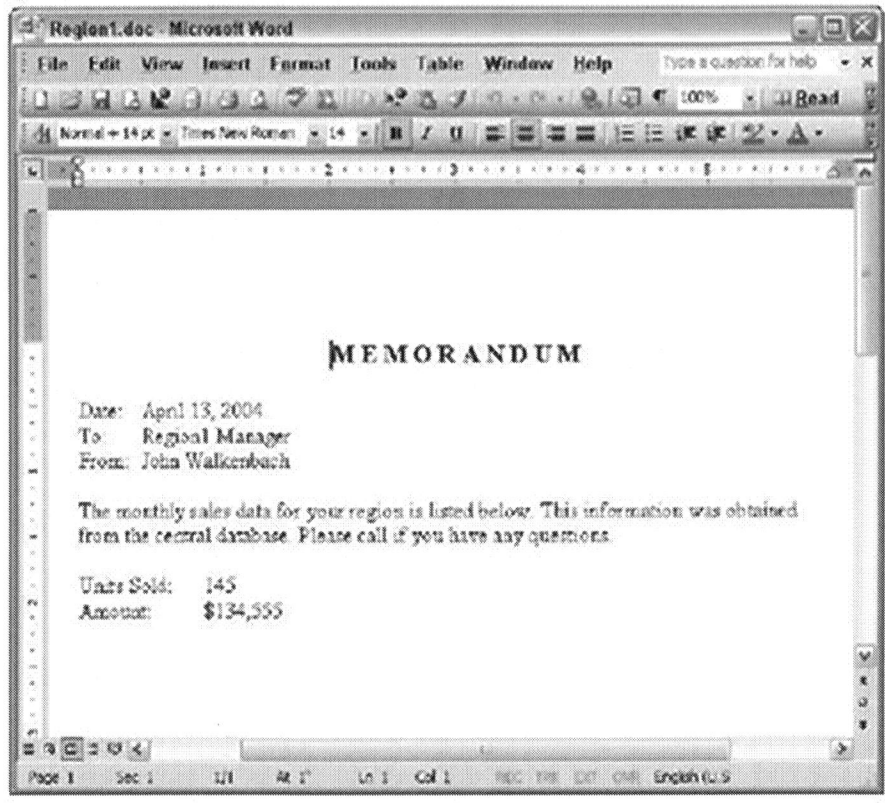

Here is the Excel VBA procedure used to create the Word document. The example described in the section is that of a Word macro which created the Excel workbook object whose moniker happens to be Excel.Sheet from the existing workbook called projection.xls. This macro prompts its user for 2 values and then creates a data table with a chart and they are stored in a Word document. The initial workbook is displayed in the figure below. This procedure MakeExcelChart prompts the user for 2 values and places them in the worksheet.

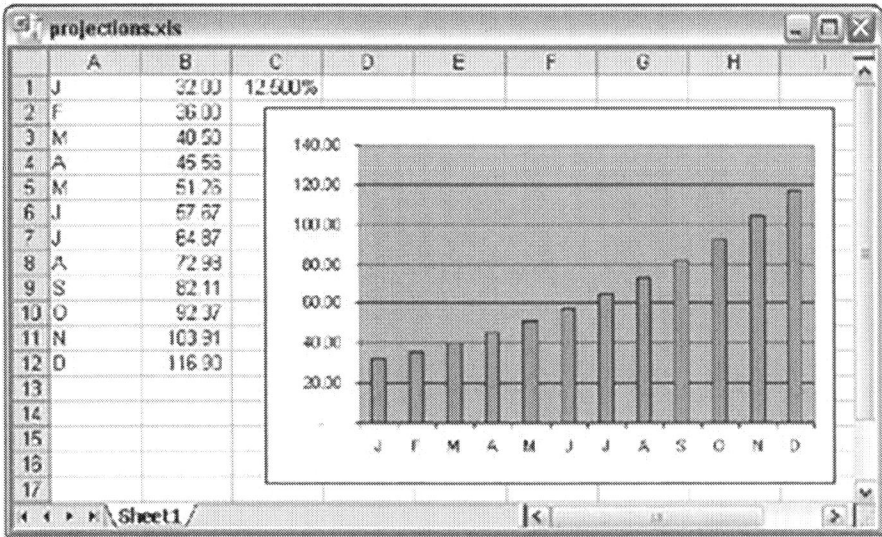

VBA procedures in Word use this type of worksheet. By recalculating the worksheet, we are updating the chart. The data and the chart are then copied from the Excel object and they are pasted in the new document. These results are displayed in the following figure.

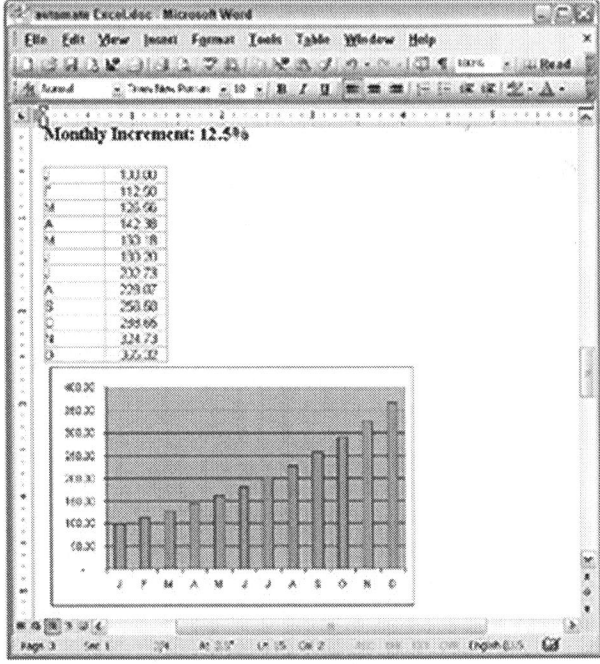

The VBA procedure from Word uses Excel for creating this document. The code used for the MakeExcelChart procedure is as follows,

```vba
Sub MakeExcelChart()
    Dim XLSheet As Object
    Dim StartVal, PctChange
    Dim Wbook As String

    '   Create a new document
    Documents.Add

    '   Prompt for values
    StartVal = InputBox("Starting Value?")
    PctChange = InputBox("Percent Change?")

    '   Create Sheet object
    Wbook = ThisDocument.Path & "\projections.xls"
    Set XLSheet = GetObject(Wbook, "Excel.Sheet").ActiveSheet

    '   Put values in sheet
    XLSheet.Range("StartingValue") = StartVal
    XLSheet.Range("PctChange") = PctChange
    XLSheet.Calculate
```

```vba
    '   Insert page heading
    Selection.Font.Size = 14
    Selection.Font.Bold = True
    Selection.TypeText "Monthly Increment: " & _
        Format(PctChange, "0.0%")
    Selection.TypeParagraph
    Selection.TypeParagraph

    '   Copy data from sheet & paste to document
    XLSheet.Range("data").Copy
    Selection.Paste

    '   Copy chart and paste to document
    XLSheet.ChartObjects(1).Copy
    Selection.PasteSpecial _
        Link:=False, _
        DataType:=wdPasteMetafilePicture, _
        Placement:=wdInLine, DisplayAsIcon:=False

    '   Kill the object
    Set XLSheet = Nothing
End Sub
```

Sending Personalized emails by using Outlook

This example in this section shows automation by using MS Outlook. The code used creates personalized email messages with the use of the data stored in the worksheet. The screenshot below shows a worksheet which contains the data used for email messages such as bonus amount, name, and email address. The procedure loops through the worksheet rows and retrieves the data. It will not stop at that and will create an individualized email message. Actually the message is stored in the Msg variable.

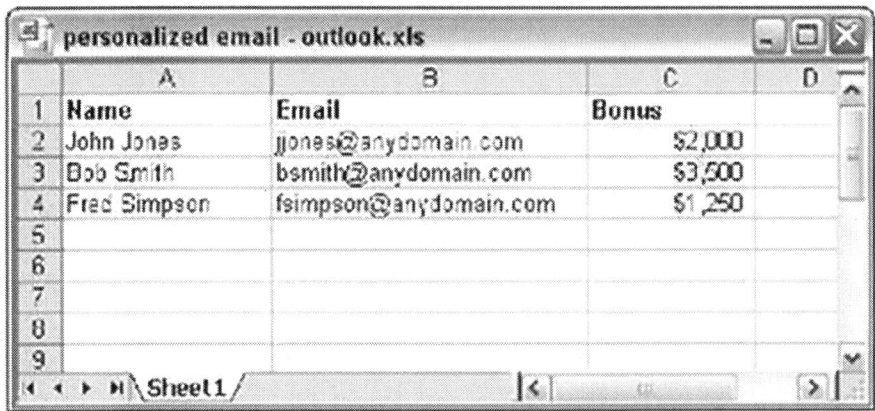

The stored info is used by Outlook Express for email messages. The next example uses Display method which only displays the email messages. In order to actually send the messages, you can rather use the Send method.

```
Sub SendEmail()
   Dim OutlookApp As Object
   Dim MItem As Object
   Dim cell As Range
   Dim Subj As String
   Dim EmailAddr As String
   Dim Recipient As String
   Dim Bonus As String
   Dim Msg As String

   'Create Outlook object
   Set OutlookApp = CreateObject("Outlook.Application")

   'Loop through the rows
   For Each cell In _
      Columns("B").Cells.SpecialCells(xlCellTypeConstants)
      If cell.Value Like "*@*" Then
         'Get the data
         Subj = "Your Annual Bonus"
         Recipient = cell.Offset(0, -1).Value
         EmailAddr = cell.Value
         Bonus = Format(cell.Offset(0, 1).Value, "$0,000.")

         'Compose message
         Msg = "Dear " & Recipient & vbCrLf & vbCrLf
         Msg = Msg & "I am pleased to inform you that "
         Msg = Msg & "your annual bonus is "
         Msg = Msg & Bonus & vbCrLf & vbCrLf
         Msg = Msg & "William Rose" & vbCrLf
         Msg = Msg & "President"

         'Create Mail Item and send it
         Set MItem = OutlookApp.CreateItem(0)
         With MItem
            .To = EmailAddr
            .Subject = Subj
            .Body = Msg
            .Display
         End With
      End If
   Next
End Sub
```

Note that here two objects are involved viz MailItem and Outlook. Outlook object is created using this statement,

```
Set OutlookApp = CreateObject("Outlook.Application")
```

128

The MailItem object gets created by using this statement,

```
Set MItem = OutlookApp.CreateItem(0)
```

The code here will set the Subject, To, and Body properties. It will then use the Send method for sending every message. The next screenshot shows one of the emails developed by Excel,

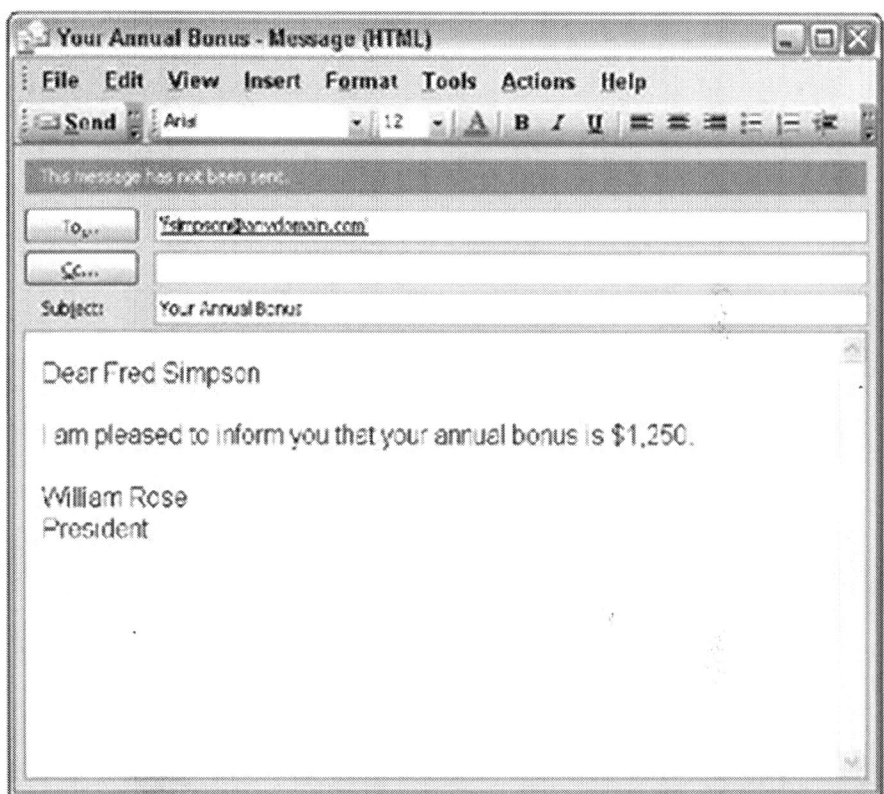

You can create personalized emails using Excel. For using this example available online, you need to install MS Outlook.

Using the ADO

The ADO or ActiveX Data Objects is an object model which empowers you to reach data that is stored in a range of database formats. It allows you to use single object models for all the databases. Here in the section, we will see a simple example of using ADO for retrieving data from your Access database. The ADO programming is a complicated topic. If you are required to reach external data in Excel, you can read more about it online with specific topics dedicated to this in detail. The example quoted here is for getting a feel of how things work.

This following example will retrieve data from the Access DB which is named budget.mdb. The database contains one table called Budget that covers 7 fields. The example retrieves data from the item field which has text, "Lease" and its Division field contains text "N. America". Qualifying data, in this case, is stored in the Recordset object and the data then gets transferred to a worksheet.

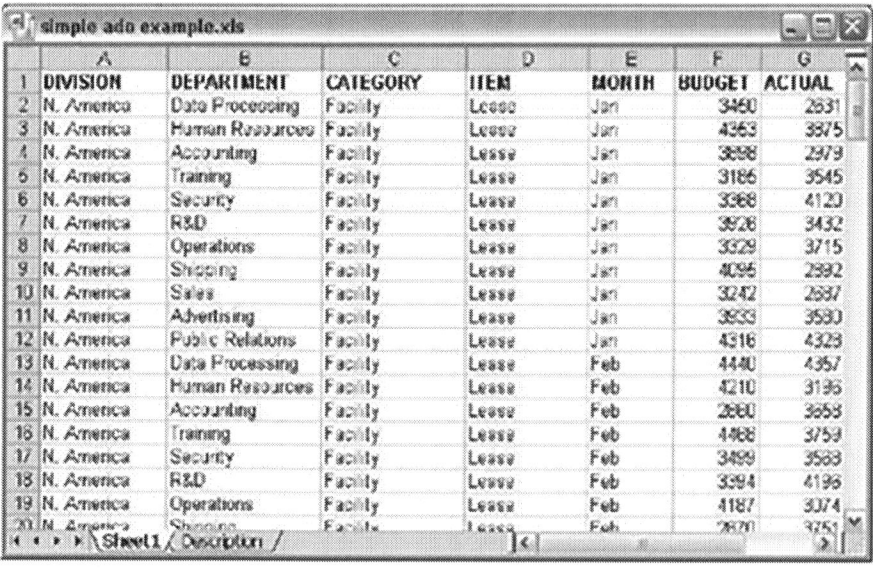

Retrieving data from your Access database,

```vb
Sub ADO_Demo()
'    This demo requires a reference to
'    the Microsoft ActiveX Data Objects 2.x Library

    Dim DBFullName As String
    Dim Cnct As String, Src As String
    Dim Connection As ADODB.Connection
    Dim Recordset As ADODB.Recordset
    Dim Col As Integer

    Cells.Clear

'    Database information
    DBFullName = ThisWorkbook.Path & "\budget.mdb"

'    Open the connection
    Set Connection = New ADODB.Connection
    Cnct = "Provider=Microsoft.Jet.OLEDB.4.0; "
    Cnct = Cnct & "Data Source=" & DBFullName & ";"
    Connection.Open ConnectionString:=Cnct
```

```vb
'    Create RecordSet
    Set Recordset = New ADODB.Recordset
    With Recordset
'        Filter
        Src = "SELECT * FROM Budget WHERE Item = 'Lease' "
        Src = Src & "and Division = 'N. America'"
        .Open Source:=Src, ActiveConnection:=Connection

'        Write the field names
        For Col = 0 To Recordset.Fields.Count - 1
            Range("A1").Offset(0, Col).Value = _
                Recordset.Fields(Col).Name
        Next

'        Write the recordset
        Range("A1").Offset(1, 0).CopyFromRecordset Recordset
    End With
    Set Recordset = Nothing
    Connection.Close
    Set Connection = Nothing
End Sub
```

Unlike the other examples cited in the chapter, this procedure makes use of early binding. So, it needs a reference to MS ActiveX Data Objects 2.0 library. You can use Tool References in the VBE for creating this reference.

131

Chapter 10

Miscellaneous Topics

Running a macro when some cells are changed in Excel

In MS Excel, you can create macros that are called only when a value is entered in a cell on a specific sheet or in any worksheet that is open at the moment. Notice that you must not call the macros unnecessarily as they slow down Excel performance. In many cases, the macro runs only when some of the cells have values entered in the cell of a sheet. You need to check to see if ActiveCell is one such key. For doing this, make use of the Intersect method over the ActiveCell and the range containing your key cells for verifying the ActiveCell as one of the key cells. In the case, ActiveCell is within the range and contains the key cells, you may call the macro. For creating the VB macro,

1. Right-click on the Sheet1 tab and then click on the ViewCode. When you do this, the Module sheet behind the Sheet1 gets opened.

2. Type this code in the module sheet,

```
Private Sub Worksheet_Change(ByVal Target As Range)

    Dim KeyCells As Range


    ' The variable KeyCells contains the cells that will

    ' cause an alert when they are changed.
```

```
Set KeyCells = Range("A1:C10")


    If Not Application.Intersect(KeyCells,
    Range(Target.Address)) _

        Is Nothing Then

        ' Display a message when one of the designated cells has
    been

        ' changed.

        ' Place your code here.

        MsgBox "Cell " & Target.Address & " has changed."

        End If

    End Sub
```

3. Now click on the "Close and Return to Microsoft Excel" available on the File menu.

Macro Error Trapping and Handling

You need the code to include in all the macros for intercepting and processing errors if and when they are occurring. Errors occur during the macro execution because of a range of reasons such as the use of incorrect code and the macro running in circumstances that were not intended originally while creating the macro. When you include error trapping in the macro, it allows you to determine what will happen when the error occurs. You gain control over the error and you are in a position to take appropriate actions without the users getting a hint that there could be something wrong.

Failure with adding the error handling will result in an undesirable and unwelcome Excel behavior. In the worst case scenario, your users may have to face a loss of recent changes in the worksheets or loss of data or Excel freezing and refusing to function. And even all of that could happen at the same time. One thing is certain and that is you want to avoid leaving the users selecting their own responses to the messages like this,

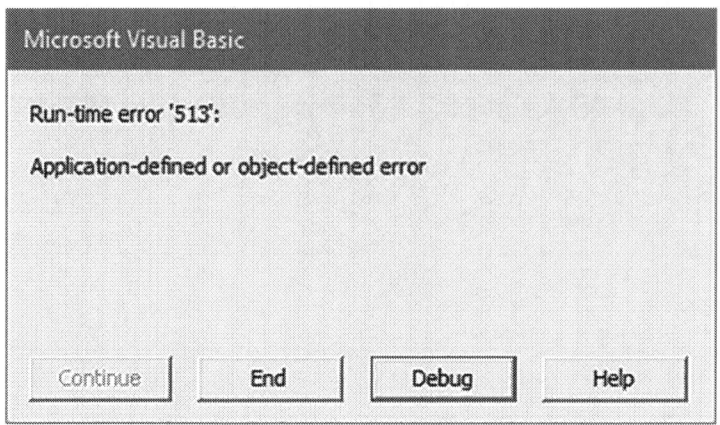

Simple Error Handling

There are many ways in which you can choose to include code for error handling inside a macro. One of them is this easy skeleton code,

Sub *YourMacroName()*

'~~~~~~

On Error Goto errHandler

your macro code here

procDone:

Exit Sub

errHandler:

MsgBox Err.Number & ": " & Err.Description

Resume procDone

End Sub

Here the On Error statement will turn on the error trapping. Information about all the errors which occur after the statement is stored in the VBA error object and it is called Err. In the event an error occurs, the "On Error Goto errHandler" statement will tell the macro to stop executing the code at the point at which this error has occurred. And then pick it up again at the errHandler label.

The "MsgBox Err.Number & ": " & Err.Description" will send a message box on the screen displaying information regarding the nature of the error. Err.Number is the unique identification number of the error object and is drawn from the VBA error library. Err.Description is the description of the error. Resume procDone tells the macro to go back to executing the procDone label.

Refined Error Handling Codes

Let's assume that you have wrapped the new macro in your error-handling code detailed above. When you test the macro, an error occurs. So now you have a message box which tells you the error number and the nature of your error. You will be in a position to revise the error handler for responding to the specific errors. In this particular example, the error number is 1234.

Sub *YourMacroName()*

'~~~~~~

On Error Goto errHandler

your macro code here

procDone:

Exit Sub

errHandler:

Select Case Err.Number

Case 1234

your code for handling error 1234

Case Else

' All outstanding errors

MsgBox Err.Number & ": " & Err.Description

End Select

Resume procDone

End Sub

When you test the macro to uncover other possible errors, you may extend the Select Case statement with the inclusion of other Cases suitably. In the following, refinement of the macro messages to your users are more specific,

Sub *YourMacroName()*

'~~~~~~

On Error Goto errHandler

Dim msg$, title$, icon&

your macro code here

procDone:

Exit Sub

errHandler:

icon& = vbOKOnly + vbCritical

Select Case Err.Number

Case 53

title$ = "Missing File"

msg$ = "Macro cannot locate an essential file."

msg$ = msg$ & vbNewline & vbNewLine

msg$ = msg$ & "Please notify the developer."

Case Else

title$ = "Unanticipated Error"

msg$ = Err.Number & ": " & Err.Description

msg$ = msg$ & vbNewline & vbNewLine

msg$ = msg$ & "Please make a note of this message"

End Select

MsgBox Err.Number & ": " & Err.Description

Resume procDone

End Sub

If you wish the user to get a message when your macro has completed its running then a further modification or refinement of the code is necessary.

Sub *YourMacroName()*

'〜〜〜〜〜〜〜〜〜〜〜〜〜〜〜〜〜〜〜〜〜〜〜〜〜〜〜〜〜〜〜〜〜〜〜〜〜〜〜

On Error Goto errHandler

Dim msg$, title$, icon&

your macro code here

title$="Macro Run Completed"

msg$ = "Please continue using the workbook"

icon& = vbOKOnly + vbExclamation

procDone:

MsgBox msg$, icon&, title$

Exit Sub

errHandler:

icon& = vbOKOnly + vbCritical

Select Case Err.Number

Case 53

title$ = "Missing File"

msg$ = "Macro cannot locate an essential file."

msg$ = msg$ & vbNewline & vbNewLine

msg$ = msg$ & "Please notify the developer."

Case Else

title$ = "Unanticipated Error"

msg$ = Err.Number & ": " & Err.Description

msg$ = msg$ & vbNewline & vbNewLine

msg$ = msg$ & "Please make a note of this message."

End Select

Resume procDone

End Sub

Debugging the macro

Error Message and the Debug Button

While you are trying to run a macro, occasionally you will get an error message like, "Run-time Error '9': Subscript out of range" as shown below. On the error message, there are three buttons available, End, Help, and Debug. For stopping the macro, press the End button. For getting more information about the error, click Help button. By doing this, you will end up on a page on the MS site having a list of probable causes and its solutions for the error Subscript out of range. If you wish to go to VBE and solve the issue, click on the Debug button.

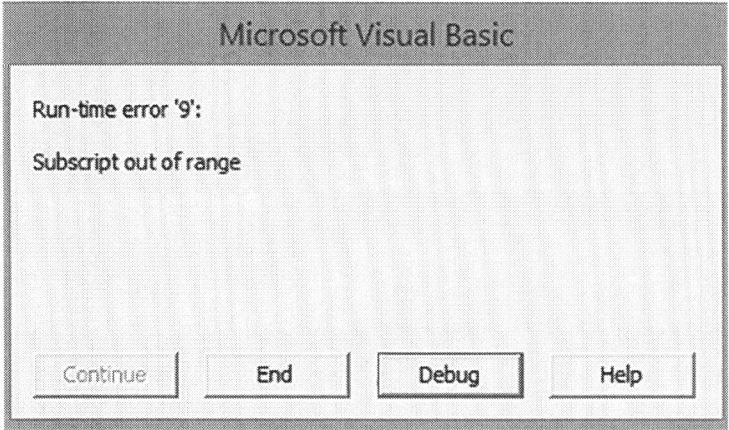

Debugging the Macro

In the example below, a macro was recorded in order to get a worksheet called "Main". Then move on to select a cell C3 from the worksheet. When you run this macro, the error message above will appear. Here is your VBA code for this GoToMainSheet macro.

```
Sub GoToMainSheet()

' GoToMainSheet Macro

    Sheets("Main").Select

    Range("C3").Select

End Sub
```

We will use the Debug button for troubleshooting the issue. In the subsequent error message, we will click the Debug button. This will open VBE and show the GoToMainSheet macro. The line of code in question will be highlighted in yellow and a yellow arrow will appear in the left margins.

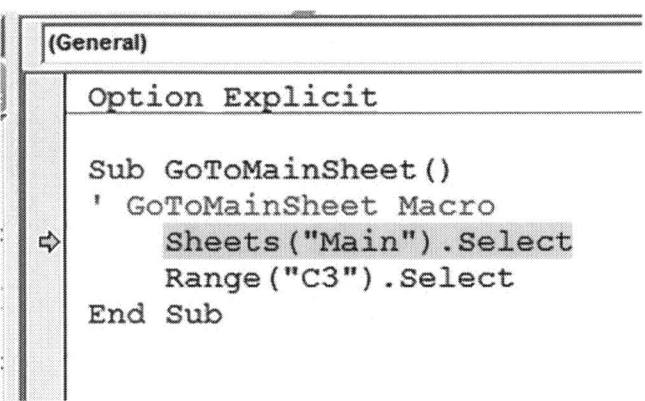

```
(General)

    Option Explicit

    Sub GoToMainSheet()
    ' GoToMainSheet Macro
⇨       Sheets("Main").Select
        Range("C3").Select
    End Sub
```

Excel displayed the error message as it cannot complete the highlighted code. Now take a look at the Project Explorer window and check out the list of sheets for active workbooks. You can find 3 sheets called Intro, Sheet2 and Sheet3 and there is no sheet called "Main".

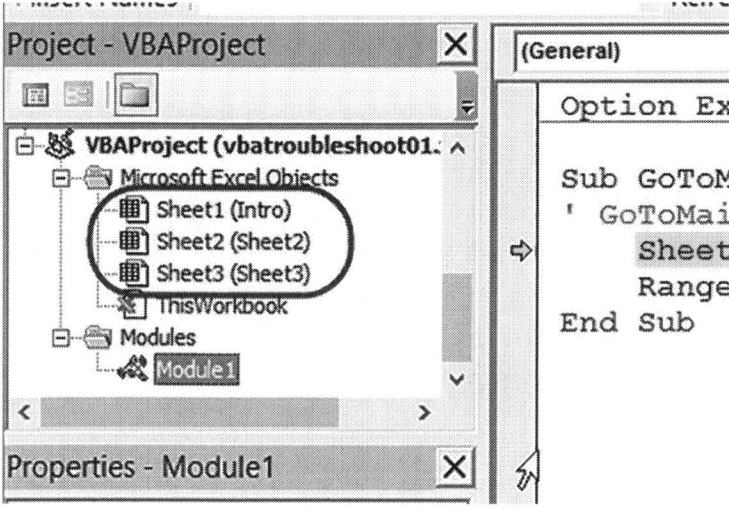

Now we will stop running the debugger and fix this code. On this VBE toolbar press the Reset button.

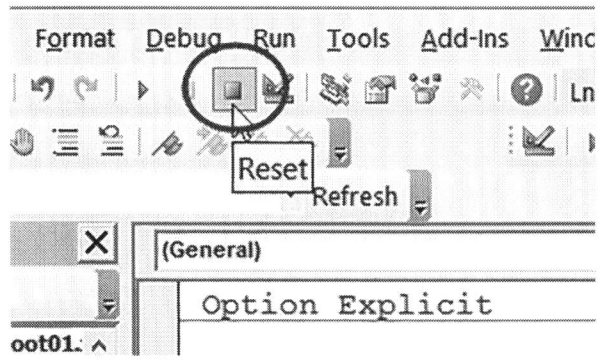

This will make the code stop running and the yellow highlighting will go away.

Fixing the code

Now you will edit the code and change the sheet name.

Solution 1: (This is not recommended)

In the code, you need to replace "Main" with "Intro" which is the correct and current name for the first sheet in your workbook. But with this solution, code will show the error again if anyone is to change the name of the sheet in future.

Sheets("Intro").Select

It is not the best solution so not recommended.

Solution 2: (This is recommended)

Rather than using the name from your Sheet tab, you will make use of the Sheet's Code Name. This is unlikely to get changed by anyone other than the programmer. You can find the Code Name of the sheet in the Project Explorer followed by the name which appears on your sheet tab.

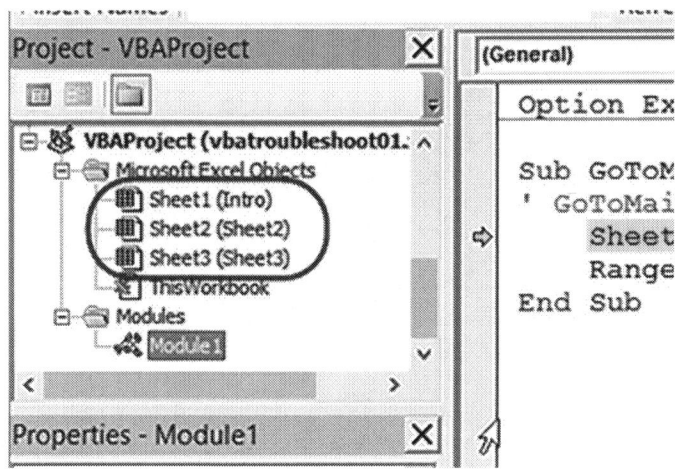

The Code Name for the first sheet is "Sheet1" so, make changes in the code for using the name.

Sheet1.Select

This is a better solution as the code will keep on running even though the name on your sheet tab is changed. Now save these changes and test your macro. On your VBE toolbar, press the Save button and close the VBE window to return to Excel. Now run your macro again to see it running correctly without displaying errors.

Using F8 to stop working

While debugging the Excel VBA code, you may use the F8 key or the Step Into command for stepping through your code one line at a time.

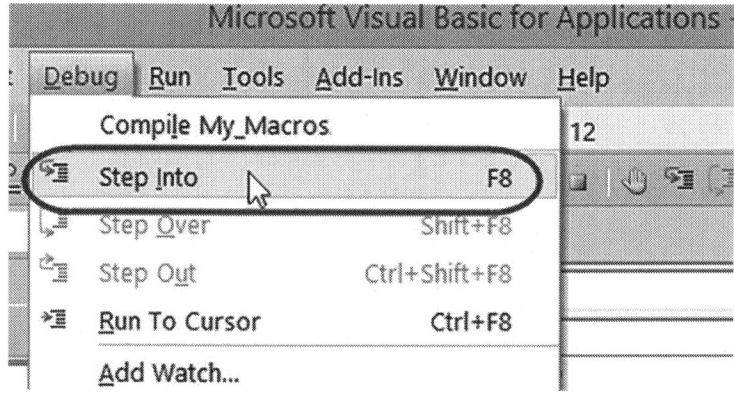

But while using Excel 2010, you may face the issue when F8 key (or the Step Into) stops working partially through the procedure. Many times this will happen when the code will open other files. Rather than stopping the next lines of code, it will run to the end of procedures or to your next breakpoint. In order to fix the issue, you will make the following changes to the Registry. Like every time, take backup of the Registry before making any modifications and remember, try this at your own risk. The changes in the Registry will affect RPC debugging and you read more about it on the MS website.

1. Now close Excel.

2. Take the backup of your Registry file and then open the Registry. These instructions can be found on the Microsoft website.

3. Go to the relevant Registry key,

For 32-bit Office on 64-bit Window select the registry key:

HKEY_LOCAL_MACHINE\SOFTWARE\Wow6432Node\Microsoft\ VBA

For 32-bit Office on 32-bit Window select the registry key:

HKEY_LOCAL_MACHINE\SOFTWARE\ Microsoft\VBA

For 64-bit Office on 64-bit Windows select the registry key:

HKEY_LOCAL_MACHINE\SOFTWARE\ Microsoft\VBA

Note that if you cannot find any of these keys, perform a search in your Registry Editor. Go to Edit -> Search for getting to Microsoft\VBA.

4. Right click on the window towards the right and press New.

5. Here, click on DWORD (You can see from the screenshot below that DWORD is for your 32-bit Office running on your 64-bit computer.)

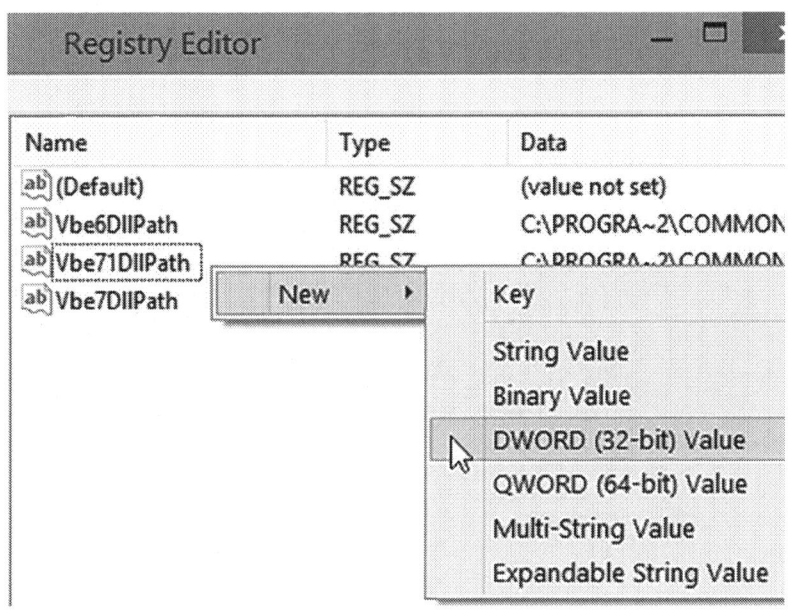

6. Name this DWORD as DisableOrpcDebugging7.

7. Now right-click on the DWORD and then click Modify.

8. Change its value to 1 and click on OK.

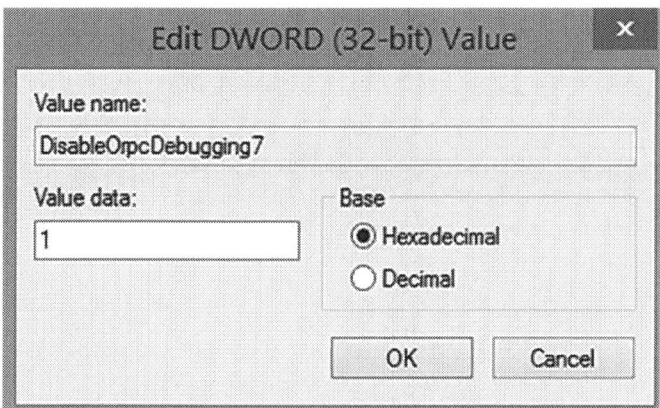

9. This will make the completed DWORD appear in your Registry.

10. Now close the Registry and go to Excel. Here your F8 key will now work properly and will step through the code.

Project Explorer folder is missing

While you are working on the VBE, the Project Explorer is normally visible and will show a list of all your open VBA projects. Now click the + or - button available on the left of your project name for opening and closing the list of objects for the project.

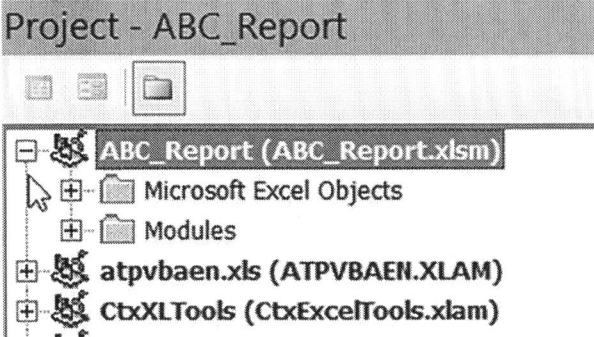

Note that when a project is protected and has not been unlocked during its current session you will get prompted for a password if you click the + button. ·

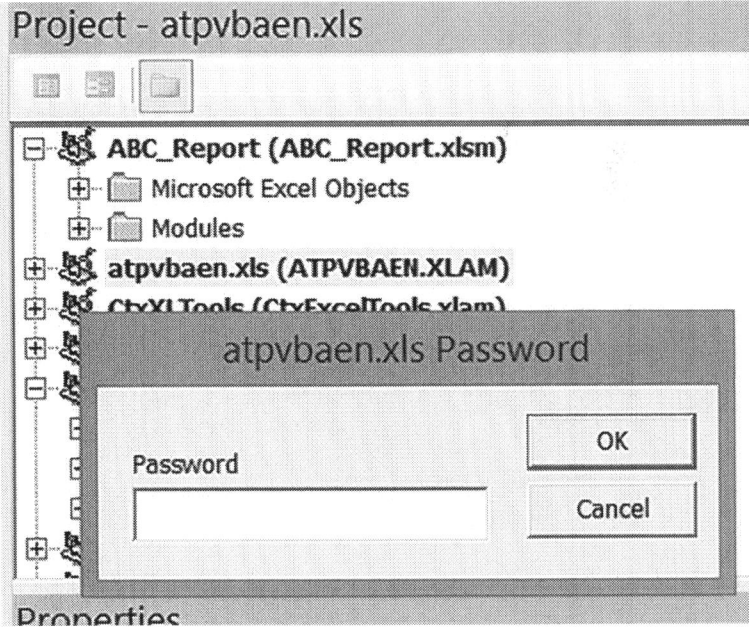

Showing Folder Contents

Now click on the + or - button on the left of your folder name for opening and closing the list of objects in the folder.

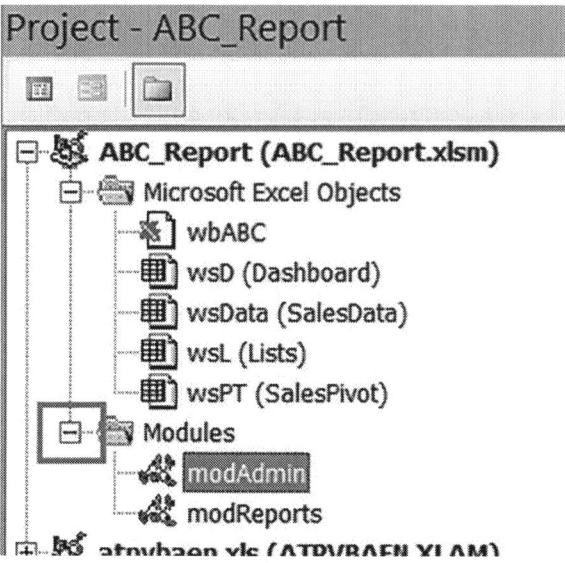

Sometimes the folders in Project Explorer go missing. In this case, the alphabetical list of the workbook objects appears below your project name.

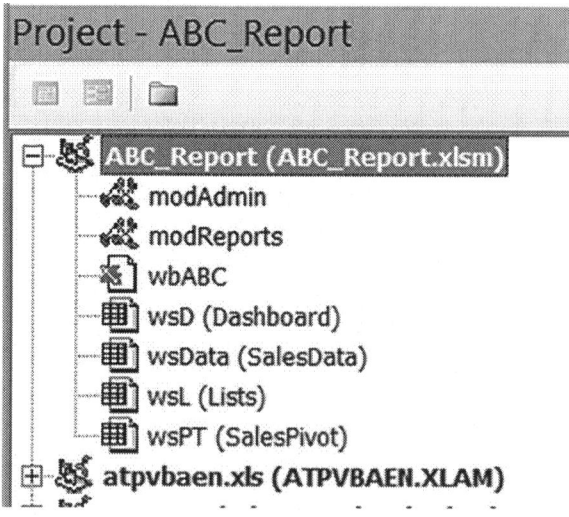

146

In order to show the objects as grouped in the folders again, use the following steps,

1. Click on Project name for unlocking a project.

2. In your toolbar which is at the top of your Project Explorer window, there is a Toggle Folders button. Click on it.

This will make the folders reappear for all projects with the objects grouping in the folders.

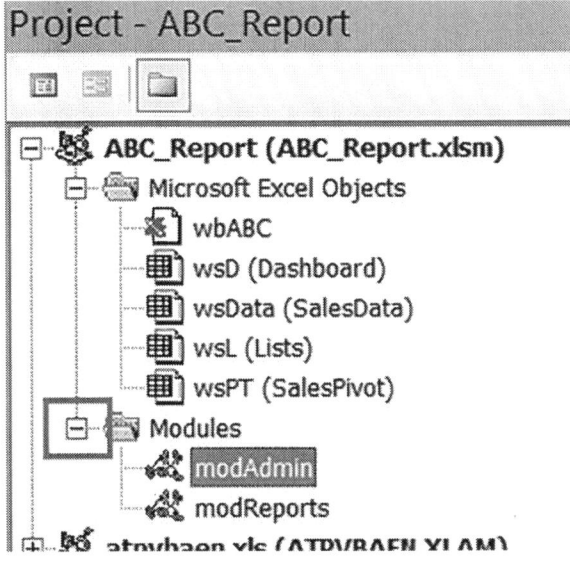

Finding Macros in Microsoft Excel 2007, 2010, 2013, 2016 and 2019

As we know, macros are used for repetitive tasks in Microsoft Excel. For those users that used Excel 2003 and are keen on using macros, it is a little difficult while using the later versions of Excel as they use Ribbons. Here are two ways of finding out the macros from earlier versions of Excel. You can then take the option of working under the classical style or use the new interface for your work.

Now let's see where to find macros in Excel 2010 and 2013.

Finding this feature on the classic menu

Open the MS Excel and click the Menus tab. This way you can retrieve the classic styled interface. After this, go to your Tools menu and you will find your Macro function listed on the dropdown menu.

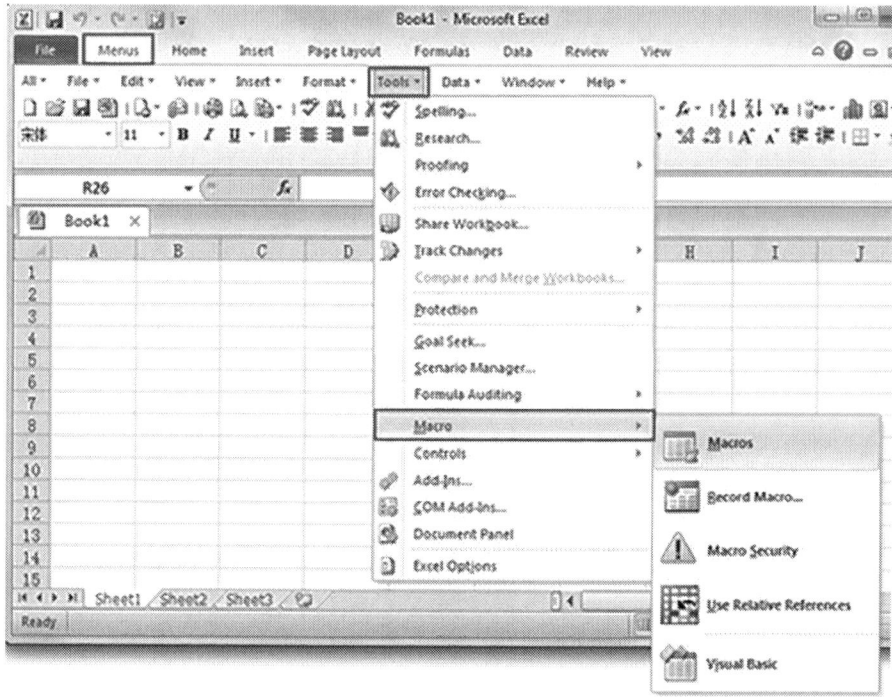

Finding the feature using the Ribbon interface

If you do not have the classic menu for Excel 2007/2010/2013/2016/2019 installed on your PC, you may open Excel and go to the View tab. Click on it and you will find the option to use Macros. From here you may manage the macro performance easily.

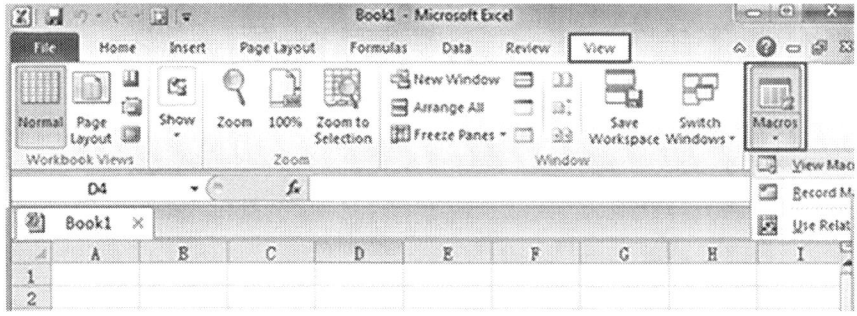

Viewing macros in Excel 2016

First you need to see the Developer tab. For this, go to the File menu from the menu bar and select Options from its dropdown menu. As the Excel Options window appears, click on the Customize Ribbon available on the left. Clicking on the Menus tab makes that classical style interface available. Then all you need to do is go to the Tools menu and you can find the Macro function listed in the dropdown.

Finding and Deleting Macros in Excel

For finding and deleting the macros follow these steps,

1. Press the Alt+F11 for displaying your VBA Editor.

2. From the Project Explorer which is available in the upper left corner of the Editor, right click on the module you wish to delete.

3. Select the Remove option from your Context menu.

4. When prompted, if you wish to export a module before removing it, click on No.

Here we will see how to remove a macro from the MS Excel spreadsheet. This can be done from within the Settings on the spreadsheet in both Windows and Mac computers.

Method 1: On Windows

1. Open the Excel sheet but it must be macro enabled. Double-click on the Excel file that contains the macro you are looking to delete. It will open the file in Excel.

2. Click on Enable Content. It is available in the yellow bar at the top of your Excel window. It will enable the macros which are embedded in the file. If you do not enable the macros, you will not be able to delete them.

3. Click on the View tab. The tab is available in the green ribbon available at the top of your Excel window.

4. Click on Macros. It is a dropdown icon on the far-right side of your View tab. You will find a dropdown menu here.

5. Click on View Macros. The option is available in the dropdown menu. This will open the macros popup-up window.

6. Click on the "Macros in" dropdown box. You can find it at the window bottom. It will prompt to a dropdown menu.

7. Click on All Open Workbooks. It is available in the dropdown menu.

8. Select the macro. Click on the macro you wish to delete.

9. Click on "Delete". It is available on the right side of your window.

10. When prompted, click on "yes". By doing this, you will remove the macro from the workbook.

11. Save the changes by pressing Ctrl+S. This will ensure that the macro remains deleted when you close Excel.

Method 2: On Mac

1. Open your macro-enabled Excel worksheet. Double click on the Excel file that contains the macro you wish to delete. It will open this file in Excel.

2. Click on Enable Content. This option is available in the yellow bar at the top of your Excel window. It will enable the macro which is embedded in your file. As we know, if the macro is not enabled, it is not possible to delete it.

3. Click on Tools. This is a menu item at the Mac screen top. Clicking this item prompts a dropdown menu.

4. Select the Macro. The option is available at the bottom of your Tools dropdown menu. Choosing it will cause the pop-up menu to appear on the right side of the dropdown menu.

5. Click on Macros. It is the pop-out menu and doing this will open Macros window.

6. Click on the Macros In in the dropdown box. It is available near Macros window bottom. Another dropdown menu will appear.

7. Click on All Open Workbooks. It is available in the dropdown menu.

8. Select a macro you wish to delete and click on it.

9. Click on -. It is at the bottom of the macro list.

10. When prompted click on yes. It will remove the macro.

11. Save the changes. Press ⌘ Command+S for doing so. It will ensure that the macro remains deleted when you have closed Excel.

Adding a macro to Excel

This means adding VBA code to the Excel workbook. For this, follow these instructions,

1. Open the Excel workbook.

2. Press Alt+F11 for opening the Visual Basic Editor (VBE).

3. Right click on the workbook name available on the pane "Project-VBAProject". It is at the top left corner of your editor window. Then select Insert->Module from your Context Menu.

Absolute and Relative Cell References

1. Absolute Cell References:

The MS Excel by default records all the cell references as Absolute. They are recorded in the A1 notation. It means that all the cell references which are selected explicitly refer to you and you will get the exact same result when a macro gets played back. These absolute references are useful when you are performing the same action in an identical situation every time. The second button of the toolbar toggles between recording in the Absolute mode besides recording in Relative mode. When the button is pressed, your relative references get used and when it remains as it is absolute references get utilized. For example,

1. Select the cell B2 before selecting Tools -> Macros -> Record New Macro.

2. In your Macro Name box type "Absolute".

3. Select cells "C3:C7".

4. Select a color by using your Fill Color button available on the formatting bar.

5. Now select the cells "D3:D7".

6. Select another color by using the Fill Color button available on the formatting bar.

7. Click the bold and italic buttons available on the formatting toolbar.

8. Now select cells "E3:E7".

9. Select another color by using the Fill Color button of the formatting toolbar.

10. Now press your Stop Recording button available on the Stop Recording toolbar.

If the Stop Recording toolbar has not appeared automatically when you began the recording, you may display it by picking View -> Toolbars -> Stop Recording. The recorded macro will produce the following code.

```
Sub Absolute()
    Range("C3:C7").Select
    With Selection.Interior
        .ColorIndex = 1
        .Pattern = xlSolid
    End With
    Range("D3:D7").Select
    With Selection.Interior
        .ColorIndex = 2
        .Pattern = xlSolid
    End With
    Selection.Font.Italic = True
    Range("E3:E7").Select
    With Selection.Interior
        .ColorIndex = 3
        .Pattern = xlSolid
    End With
End Sub
```

2. Relative Call References

In many cases, you will be required to record a macro by using cell references which are Relative to a specific cell. They are recorded by using the R1C1 notation. For instance, you might wish to enter some data inside the active cell and also enter some data in the cell directly below it. These relative references are useful when performing actions anywhere else on your worksheets. You may switch to relative recording mode by pressing the button on the right side of your Stop Recording toolbar. The button is a toggle and you can change between relative and absolute references anytime while recording your macro. However, remember that there is no indication given other than this button being pushed in as to which mode is currently being used. The first recorded macro inside a workbook will always begin by using an absolute reference.

If you stop recording while you were using relative references, the next recorded macro will begin with the use of relative references. Use of relative references will generate code which will always refer to a cell presently selected before you started the recording. And then it uses the "Offset" method for obtaining relative cell address. For instance,

1. Select the cell B2 before moving on and selecting Tools -> Macros -> Record New Macro.

2. Inside the Macro Name box, type "Relative".

3. Select Relative References button on your Stop Recording toolbar.

4. Repeat the exact same steps as those used in Absolute References for steps 3 to 9.

5. Click the Relative References button again for switching back to the Absolute references.

6. Now press the Stop Recording button available on Stop Recording toolbar.

The recorded macro will produce the following code,

```
Sub Relative()
    ActiveCell.Offset(1, 1).Range("A1:A5").Select
    With Selection.Interior
        .ColorIndex = 1
```

```
        .Pattern = xlSolid
    End With
    ActiveCell.Offset(0, 1).Range("A1:A5").Select
    With Selection.Interior
        .ColorIndex = 2
        .Pattern = xlSolid
    End With
    Selection.Font.Italic = True
    ActiveCell.Offset(0, 1).Range("A1:A5").Select
    With Selection.Interior
        .ColorIndex = 3
        .Pattern = xlSolid
    End With
End Sub
```

Absolute or Relative

While recording a macro, cell references are made either relative to the start position or having an absolute address. By default, the recorded macro uses absolute cell referencing. It means that the exact cell reference is recorded in the macro. You may switch back and forth between two macro recording settings. You can do it as many times as you wish. While you are recording a macro, it will be recorded with an absolute recording by default though. In order to emphasize the 2 different settings, we will perform some simple formatting of the table of data. First, we will use absolute referencing and then the relative referencing.

Most of the code, in this case, is the same, however, there is a difference between the ways the cells are selected. While you are using absolute references, selecting or moving from cells generates code which refers to the specific range of cells.

```
Range("C3:C7").Select
```

For the relative references, this code generated is a reference to another cell specific to the active cell which is the initially selected cell.

```
ActiveCell.Offset(1, 1).Range("A1:A5").Select
```

Absolute or Relative Recording

While recording your macro, it is recorded with an absolute recording by default. Here is an example of code which is recorded by using the absolute recording.

```
Range("B2").Select

ActiveCell.Value = "some text"

Range("B4").Select
```

If you select or move from a cell to another, the exactly concerned cell range will be utilized. You may go to Relative recording at any time with the use of the toggle button available on Stop Recording toolbar. Here is the example of code that is recorded by using relative referencing,

```
ActiveCell.Offset(-2,2).Range("A1").Select

ActiveCell.Value = "some text"

ActiveCell.Offset(10,-3).Range("A1").Select
```

5 Applications of Excel VBA Macros

Let's see five ways of using Excel VBA macros for automating Excel tasks you encounter frequently at work. Where can you use the macros? This happens to be the query you will encounter often. People often make a reference to the fact that you need to learn macros. However, you are not sure exactly how they will help. Here are five ways in which the macros can help you in automating tasks in Excel. We can use VBA macros for automating anything, from easy tasks to complex reporting procedures having multiple files. Here are the five topics that are covered in this chapter.

1. **Data related tasks**: The tasks related to data include everyday tasks such as cleaning up and formatting data. Some of the examples are,

- Removing duplicates and creating a list of unique values.

- Selecting or deleting blank rows.

- Creating formulas such as percentage change formula by using macros.

- Finding the last used cells, rows or columns in the worksheets.

- Applying the formatting to the raw data exports like in format copier.

2. **Workbook related tasks**: You may also program tasks across worksheets and workbooks. It includes things such as listing all the sheets, hiding specific sheets, creating a table of content, opening and closing a workbook and many more. Here are some examples used commonly,

- TOC Gallery for a table of content.

- Saving and closing all open workbooks.

3. **Pivot Table Tasks**: Pivot tables are an extremely handy feature of Excel. Although they can turn out to be very time consuming to create,

update, format and maintain. Luckily, we may automate just about all properties and actions by using the pivot tables in VBA macros. Here are some examples,

- A macro showing details.

- Automatic default number formatting by using Excel pivot tables.

- Expand and collapse all pivot table fields.

- Changing the date formatting for the grouped pivot table fields.

- Using the PivotPal Add-In. This complete add-in was built using VBA and it automates several repetitive tasks related to pivot tables.

4. **Userforms and Add-ins**: The userforms are the windows that open in Excel with interactive controls. They make the spreadsheet easy for other users to operate. Userforms can be created and modified by using the VBA Editor. The add-ins are installed on user computers and normally contain customized ribbon tabs having buttons. It allows other users to run the macros on any of the open workbooks. You can check the available add-ins online for examples.

5. **Process Automation**: It is also possible to automate more difficult and complex procedures by using macros and VBA. It includes creating systems for creation, updating, and modification of many Excel files. For example, many systems like these are created for budgeting and forecasting purposes. File manager applications can also be created by using these macros. The file manager application allows you to run many macros on a set of files.

The macros can be used for just about all the tasks that can be performed by using Excel. We are not even scratching the surface with the examples mentioned above. But it might get you thinking about automating some repetitive tasks in Excel.

Creating Excel VBA Userforms

Here we will see how to create Excel VBA userforms. The userform that we will create is to look like this,

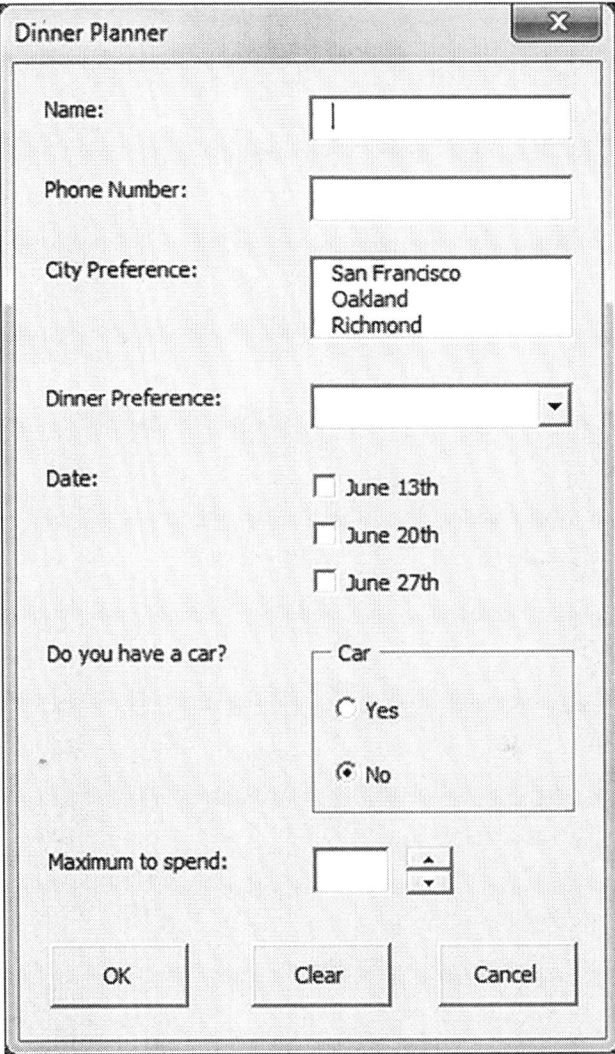

Adding the Controls

In order to add controls to the userform, perform the following steps,

1. Open your VBE (Visual Basic Editor). If the Project Explorer is not evident, click on View -> Project Explorer.

2. Click on Insert Userform. If the toolbar does not appear automatically click on View -> Toolbox. The screen will be set up like below,

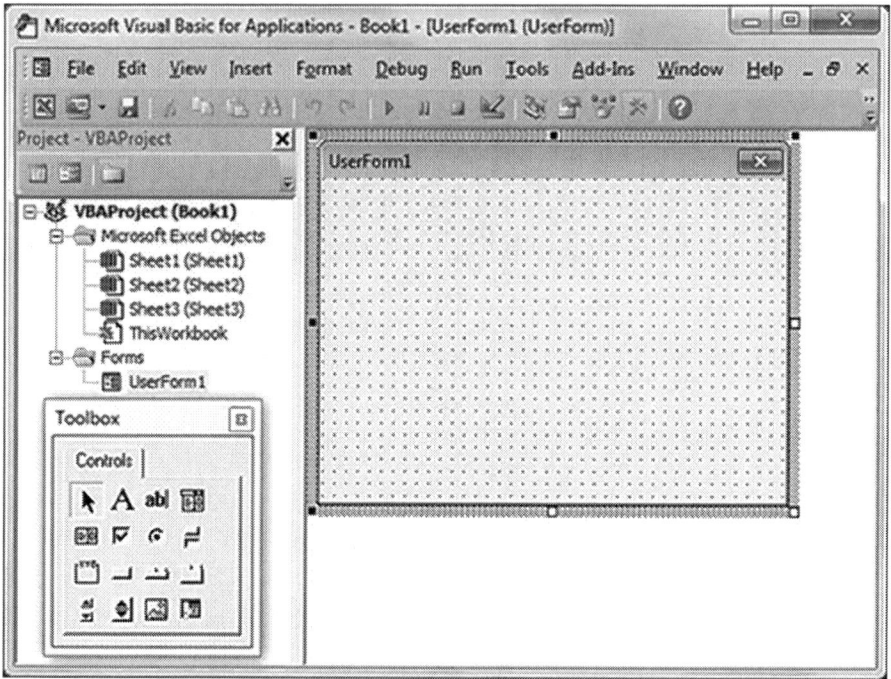

3. Now, add the controls listed below in the table. When this task is finished, the results will be consistent with the picture of userform displayed earlier. For instance, create one text box control by clicking on the TextBox from Toolbox. Now you can drag the textbox over the userform. Once you have reached the Car frame, make sure that you draw this frame first before placing the 2 option buttons in it.

4. Change the captions and names of the controls as per the table below. These names are utilized in the Excel VBA code. On the other hand, the captions are those which will appear on the screen. It is a wise thing to change the name of controls. It will make your code simpler to read. In order to change the captions and names of your controls, click on View -> Properties Window and then click on every control.

Control	Name	Caption
Userform	DinnerPlannerUserForm	Dinner Planner
Text Box	NameTextBox	
Text Box	PhoneTextBox	
List Box	CityListBox	
Combo Box	DinnerComboBox	
Check Box	DateCheckBox1	June 13th
Check Box	DateCheckBox2	June 20th
Check Box	DateCheckBox3	June 27th
Frame	CarFrame	Car
Option Button	CarOptionButton1	Yes
Option Button	CarOptionButton2	No
Text Box	MoneyTextBox	
Spin Button	MoneySpinButton	
Command Button	OKButton	OK
Command Button	ClearButton	Clear
Command Button	CancelButton	Cancel
7 Labels	No need to change	Name:, Phone Number:, etc.

Note that a combo box is a dropdown list in which a user can choose an item or fill in an item of your own choice. Remember, just one of the option buttons will be selected.

Displaying the Userform

In order to display the userform, add a command button on the worksheet and add this code,

```vba
Private Sub CommandButton1_Click()

DinnerPlannerUserForm.Show

End Sub
```

Now we will create a Sub UserForm_Initialize. Once you have made use of the Show method for your Userform, the Sub will be automatically executed. Here are the steps for this,

1. Open your VBE (Visual Basic Editor).

2. In your Project Explorer right click on the DinnerPlannerUserform and then click on View Code.

3. Select userform from your drop-down list on the left. Select Initialize from your right side drop-down list.

4. Add these code lines,

```vba
Private Sub UserForm_Initialize()
'Empty NameTextBox
NameTextBox.Value = ""


'Empty PhoneTextBox
PhoneTextBox.Value = ""


'Empty CityListBox
CityListBox.Clear
```

```vba
'Fill CityListBox
With CityListBox
    .AddItem "San Francisco"
    .AddItem "Oakland"
    .AddItem "Richmond"
End With


'Empty DinnerComboBox
DinnerComboBox.Clear


'Fill DinnerComboBox
With DinnerComboBox
    .AddItem "Italian"
    .AddItem "Chinese"
    .AddItem "Frites and Meat"
End With


'Uncheck DataCheckBoxes
DateCheckBox1.Value = False
DateCheckBox2.Value = False
DateCheckBox3.Value = False


'Set no car as default
CarOptionButton2.Value = True
```

'Empty MoneyTextBox

MoneyTextBox.Value = ""

'Set Focus on NameTextBox

NameTextBox.SetFocus

End Sub

The text boxes are made empty, list boxes and combo boxes are filled and the checkboxes remain unchecked etc.

Assigning the macros

Now that we have created the first part of userform, we move forward. Although it looks good already, nothing much will happen when we click on the command buttons of the userform. For this we need to assign the macros. Here are the steps,

1. Open the VBE (Visual Basic Editor).

2. In your Project Explorer, double click on the DinnerPlannerUserForm.

3. Now, double click on Money Spin button.

4. Now, add the following line of code,

Private Sub MoneySpinButton_Change()

MoneyTextBox.Text = MoneySpinButton.Value

End Sub

This line of code will update the textbox if you make use of the spin button.

5. Double click the OK button.

6. Add the following line of code,

```
Private Sub OKButton_Click()


Dim emptyRow As Long


'Make Sheet1 active
Sheet1.Activate


'Determine emptyRow
emptyRow = WorksheetFunction.CountA(Range("A:A")) + 1


'Transfer information
Cells(emptyRow, 1).Value = NameTextBox.Value

Cells(emptyRow, 2).Value = PhoneTextBox.Value

Cells(emptyRow, 3).Value = CityListBox.Value

Cells(emptyRow, 4).Value = DinnerComboBox.Value


If DateCheckBox1.Value = True Then Cells(emptyRow, 5).Value = DateCheckBox1.Caption


If DateCheckBox2.Value = True Then Cells(emptyRow, 5).Value = Cells(emptyRow, 5).Value & " " & DateCheckBox2.Caption
```

If DateCheckBox3.Value = True Then Cells(emptyRow, 5).Value = Cells(emptyRow, 5).Value & " " & DateCheckBox3.Caption

If CarOptionButton1.Value = True Then

    Cells(emptyRow, 6).Value = "Yes"

Else

    Cells(emptyRow, 6).Value = "No"

End If

Cells(emptyRow, 7).Value = MoneyTextBox.Value

End Sub

In the beginning we will activate Sheet1. Next, we will determine the emptyRow. This variable emptyRow is your first empty row and raises every time a record is added to it. And in the end, we will transfer the info from Userform to a specific column of emptyRow.

7. Double click on Clear button.

8. Add this lines of code,

Private Sub ClearButton_Click()

Call UserForm_Initialize

End Sub

This line of code calls your Sub UserForm_Initialize when you have clicked on the Clear button.

9. Double click on Cancel button.

10. Add the following lines of code,

Private Sub CancelButton_Click()

Unload Me

End Sub

The line of code closes the UserForm once you click the Cancel button. Now exit the VBE and enter the labels as shown below in the row 1 to test the userform.

▲	A	B	C	D	E	F	G
1	Name	Phone Number	City	Dinner	Date	Car	Maximum to spend
2	Niels	070 540 546	Oakland	Chinese	June 13th	No	30
3	Bregje	070 748 847	San Francisco	Italian	June 13th June 20th	Yes	40
4							
5							.

Some additional reasons for creating and using macros

For many beginners, macros are the scariest part of the Excel learning process. Agreed that VBA takes care of pretty much all the punctuation marks and typos but the Excel macros can also improve the productivity significantly with proper instructions. Here are some additional reasons for creating macros,

1. We live in the world of Excel: In case you pride yourself on the fact that you have memorized all the ALT keyboard shortcuts for formatting each and every paste you need then you are living in the world of Excel. Rather than using the keyboard shortcuts that do one thing, why not have shortcuts that will do many things? For instance, the Delete key clears the content of a cell but the cell formatting and comments remain. You can have a simple macro for this which will perform all 3 tasks, clearing the content, formatting and commenting where Ctrl keyboard shortcut is used.

167

2. You can definitely use an assistant: You may be very quick at setting up new sheets with all the right headings or copying the previous month's sheet to create a new one, but you may be able to do better things with your time. Right? In some cases, there is no need to even know VBA for creating macros that will automate tedious procedures. The recorder can do this for you. So, macros will work faster than any human assistance that can be provided.

3. You can import text files regularly: In case you are looking to import text files regularly, you may create a macro for the purpose with a little bit of macro knowledge. But if you are looking to import different files every time then creating the macros will need more work.

Conclusion

The question on everyone's mind will be, what is the future of Excel and VBA macros in this fast-changing world of technology? Well, rest assured that Excel VBA macros will be here until you are retired. Microsoft is aware that there are millions of organizations out there that depend on millions of macros made via Excel. They might have changed to other languages but those VBA macros will work for them no matter, for many decades to come on the PC and the Mac.

The reason for this confidence is that Microsoft still supports Excel 4 macros after 20 years since they became functionally outdated. Excel 4 comes with a primitive macro language which was introduced in August 1992 but was taken out of action by VBA in the next version Excel 5 in June 1994. Excel 4 was not used by many people for programming because it was not very user-friendly. But those programs still ran in Excel 2016 as Microsoft knew that many companies still depended on them.

Microsoft has now decided that VBA is not to be extended to a platform that already does not have it. Therefore there will not be any macros for the iPhone, iPad or Android devices. Rather they are developing a macro language which is based on JavaScript and it is to be extended to Windows, Mac, Android, iOS and Excel Online. You may start building macros by using JavaScript even now but it will not be fun as they still do not have a macro recorder, objects, methods, and properties. It is still incomplete and evolving with a syntax that is not user-friendly and less readable than VBA.

Another problem is that JavaScript does not support 2D arrays. You need to use arrays of arrays instead. This language runs asynchronously, therefore, you will have to design the code yourself. And it is slow but, if you are looking for a macro to run on the iPad, this is the path to take going forward.

References

Chapter 3:

https://www.makeuseof.com/tag/vba-macros-excel-tutorial/

Chapter 5:

http://www.excelitems.com/2010/12/optimize-vba-code-for-faster-macros.html

Chapter 6:

https://powerspreadsheets.com/excel-macro-tutorial-for-beginners/

Chapter 7:

https://www.excelcampus.com/vba/excel-vba-macro-shortcuts/#1

Chapter 8:

https://powerspreadsheets.com/excel-vba-tutorial-essential-terms/#Macro-Example-Horse-Sugar-Cubes

Chapter 9:

http://what-when-how.com/excel-vba/interacting-with-other-office-applications-via-excel-vba/

Chapter 10

https://support.microsoft.com/en-us/help/213612/how-to-run-a-macro-when-certain-cells-change-in-excel

http://www.consultdmw.com/excel-macro-error-handling.html

https://www.contextures.com/excelvbatips.html

https://bettersolutions.com/excel/macros/absolute-or-relative.htm

https://www.excel-easy.com/vba/userform.html